FATHERHOOD

FATHERHOOD

Brian Jackson

London
GEORGE ALLEN & UNWIN
Boston   Sydney

George Allen & Unwin (Publishers) Ltd,
40 Museum Street, London WC1A 1LU

George Allen & Unwin (Publishers) Ltd,
Park Lane, Hemel Hempstead, Herts HP2 4TE, UK

Allen & Unwin Inc.,
9 Winchester Terrace, Winchester, Mass 01890, USA

George Allen & Unwin Australia Pty Ltd,
8 Napier Street, North Sydney, NSW 2060, Australia

First published in 1984

British Library Cataloguing in Publication Data

Jackson, Brian, 1932–1983
  Fatherhood.
1. Fathers
I. Title
306.8'742   HQ756
ISBN 0-04-649025-6

Set in 10 on 11 point Palatino by Grove Graphics, Tring, Hertfordshire
and printed in Great Britain by Billing and Sons Ltd,
London and Worcester

For Seth
my seven-year-old son

who burst in as I finally put down my pen, and, trampling all over the scattered manuscript on the floor, said:

'Jumping jelly babies. Don't say you've finished work at last. Now you can play cricket with me on the Downs — and I bat first.'

Contents

Acknowledgements

I once sat in front of an old mill owner's fireplace in the West Riding of Yorkshire. Around the chimney breast, in gilded art nouveau lettering, was an entwined motto. It read: 'Everyman's Chimney is his Golden Milestone.' I leave Freudian scholars to unravel the hidden codes of the Industrial Revolution; but books too, however modest, are markers on one's attempt to think about life, to stake it out, to organize the anarchy of experience, and to consider at least one facet of Everyman.

That thinking, as all know (however tortuous the task of simplification), may often be done alone, but never in a vacuum: and writing makes one freshly aware of the gift relationship, of how much we each owe to the experience, stimulus, practicality, and spontaneous help of others. Certainly I am grateful to the Social Science Research Council and to the Child Health and Education Survey at the University of Bristol which gave me a start for this study. But of course many individuals have generously supported the notion that fathers might be a valuable and complementary study to that extraordinarily vaster literature in which we record what we know of mothers, children, the family and society.

In the United Kingdom, I am variously and differently indebted to San Last, Jacqueline Korn, Douglas Tilbe, Peter Leek, Bill and Shelagh Webb, Tilli Edelman, Margaret Carter, Barrie Knight, Hazel Wigmore, Gillian Degens, Neville Butler, John and Elizabeth Newsom, Sue Dowling, Gillian Turner; and, for space to write, to Janet Evans in Cambridge, to so many people in the village of Drewsteignton on Exmoor and in the independent settlement of Hay on Wye (undecided as to whether it is England or Wales, or neither), to my colleagues at the National Children's Centre on the banks of the Colne in Yorkshire, to Mrs Walter Raleigh Frobisher and to the Master and Fellows of St Catharine's College, Cambridge.

In the United States I owe particular thanks to Bob Paul of Concord, Jerry Bruner of Harvard, Michael Lamb of Utah, Bob and Rhona Rapoport of New York and James Levine of Bank Street; in Australia Ann Gorman, Graeme Russell and June Jeremy; in New Zealand I am always grateful for the kind and steadfast advice of

Jenni Gunby; and in the West Indies I have an especial appreciation of Dr Zulaika Ali who worked with me as the Franklyn Adams scholar in the genesis of this research.

And what can I say of Nellie, Sonia, Dominic, Christian, Rebecca, Lucy, Ellen and Seth except that it is very much more pleasant being a son, husband or father than analysing that last and often overlooked role?

Brian Jackson
Bristol University, 1983

Preface

by Sonia Jackson

Brian Jackson had just completed the final revision of this book when he died. He was taking part in a Fun-Run in aid of the National Children's Centre which he founded. Seth, his youngest son and cricketing companion, was beside him.

Brian was a man who was apt to be described as larger than life by people who met him for the first time, but in this book he made a determined effort to keep himself in the background and to allow his hundred fathers to speak for themselves. Of course he longed to tell them how to do it, and his next book was planned to explore aspects of men's emotional life in a much more personal way: men as sons, brothers, fathers, stepfathers, grandfathers. He looked forward to being a grandfather — an utterly unexplored role, except for a few glimpses in literature, but surely of great significance, both to the child and the man. It must be a manifestation of the agism of which we are only just becoming aware that it has been so overlooked. And yet another of the dozens of schemes on Brian's desk when he died was a plan to tap the experience and skills of people over retiring age — Age Resource he called it.

People who write about children are not always blessed with happiness in their own family relations. Perhaps sometimes it is their difficulties which give them the incentive to analyse and explore what to others is non-problematic. Brian's motivation was the opposite. All around him he saw men being shunted on to the sidelines of their children's lives, perhaps not now the remote and distant figures that their own fathers had been, but still playing a peripheral role. He wanted to share his own intense pleasure in watching and helping a child's personality and abilities unfold, the physical and emotional intimacy of childhood turning into a more separate but equally loving friendship in the teenage years.

For Brian being a father was the most important of the many jobs he tackled in his life and it required just as much hard work, thought and planning as writing books or developing new projects. He concentrated as totally on a conversation with a child as with a cabinet minister. He was always late for everything, especially in the evening, because he refused to hustle a child out of its natural rhythms. That precious, peaceful hour at bedtime was not to be sacrificed, even if it did mean arriving at friends for supper breathless and apologetic halfway through the soup.

Watching him with children was a daily revelation. He could tease a two-year old into paroxysms, think of tiny surprises to wipe out a trying day at school, fascinate a teenager with politics and philosophy. He was constantly sensitive to their needs, endlessly tolerant of their awkwardness. Like his much admired friend, A. S. Neill, he never forgot what it was like to be a child, bombarded with information and instructions by grownups. Nothing is so wearisome as the parent who will let no happy minute flit by without tagging on a message. Sometimes, he said, parents need to respect the invisible signs 'Private: child doing nothing. Trespassers will be prosecuted'.

But he strongly disagreed with Neill's idea that children should be left to discover their own interests and talents. His view of parenthood was highly active. He believed parents should be given access to scientific knowledge about child development and encouraged to use it to give their own children a better start. And two earlier books *Living with Children* and *Your Exceptional Child* aim to show how that can work not just in theory but amid the unpredictable stresses and untidiness of life in a real family. He included the mistakes as well as the successes. Being a parent is something you can only learn on the job — but there is no need to start from scratch every time.

Schools he considered necessary but very insufficient. Parents have to educate their children with teachers to assist them, not the other way round, and anyway a vital chunk of education is already done before a child gets anywhere near a school.

The research on which this book is based was originally called 'The *educational* role of fathers in very early childhood'. As so often happens with real research, the emphasis of the enquiry shifted, and perhaps its most striking finding is the violent emotional impact of becoming a father on men who had learned to deny that part of themselves. What has this to do with education? To make the link we have to go back again to real families, where caring for a baby is one of dozens of daily tasks and preoccupations. Most mothers, for example, only cope as well as they do because babies can be persuaded to spend much of their day asleep. Long before modern research techniques proved him right, Brian had become convinced that babies often sleep out of boredom, losing valuable hours when they could be actively living and learning. To capitalise on that knowledge needs more resources, and where better to find them than within the family itself? At present most men only spend tiny amounts of time with their young babies; the emotional charge generated by the experience of childbirth is allowed to run into the ground, when, harnessed, it could transform our view of 'normal' child development. The educational power of fathers, especially in very early childhood, is quite unknown. Who can tell what will be the effects of releasing it?

This does not mean turning fathers into teachers like the misguided Mr Gradgrind in Dickens' 'Hard Times'. Learning for little children happens best invisibly, amidst the fun, jokes and cuddles of family life. Too often fathers still miss out on both the learning and the fun. I hope this book will help many more men to get as much joy from fatherhood as my Brian did.

S. J.
December 1983

PART ONE

On the Brink

1

The Invisible Man

This book is about one dimension of the male experience: early
fatherhood. It makes no claims, because what becomes immediately
obvious is that we know very little about fathers. This study can
be no more than a seek-and-find foray. Much of it is listen and watch
and note. Most of our recorded knowledge and images of how fathers
feel and behave is lodged in literature: Oedipus at the crossroads,
Macduff meeting the news of his children's death, Karenin holding
on to the custody of his small boy, Paul Morel seeing his mineworker
father only through the filter of his mother's estrangement. Even
autobiographies yield less than one might expect. Frequently father
is dutifully there in the opening chapter, possibly overshadowed by
mother, and then fading from the narrative at a very early stage.
We can all recall exceptions, and a multiplicity of insights, but my
initial review of both fiction and documentary was a reminder of
how remote, or at least distanced, the father figure could be; and
how infrequently the relationship with the new child was seen
through his eyes. This occurs with many of the fathers interviewed
in this book. They seldom have difficulty in recalling their sense of
a mother's relationship with them, when young. But when one asks
about their father, there is hesitation, and sometimes a first
exploration of that tract of selective memory.
  If we search for hard data about modern fatherhood in sociological
studies, once again the results are scanty, and mostly concerned with
abnormal men. Faced with this situation, I took two decisions.
Neither is perfect: they are mere beginnings. But at least they
promised to provide an entry into a stretch of common experience.
One was to concentrate on first-time fathers, and on couples where
the relationship then seemed stable and the birth unlikely to present
special problems. The medical profession usually stream their clients,

and, having picked up any physical, mental or social early warning systems, try and see if the mother can be placed under the oversight of a consultant with a particular knowledge in that field. Most pregnancies now fall in a broad band where no immediate or major difficulties are foreseen. I therefore worked with a distinguished consultant whose speciality was the normal and usually happy birth that most couples experience. Yet even a moderate-sized hospital may have several thousand births each year, and the challenge is to treat each one as a unique event. My sample was simply the next hundred men who were soon to find themselves to be first-time fathers. None of them have twins; no mother dies in childbirth; no boy or girl is born handicapped; no man is in prison, hospital or far away at sea. I sidestepped many of the dramas that might surround the entry into fatherhood, not because those are not important, but because I wanted to begin with the normal, if variegated experience of the majority. We run across these men all the time, may meet and congratulate them here and there, and perhaps count ourselves in their number. New fatherhood may be special to them but yet part of the humdrum round to the rest of us.

My second decision was to listen, rather than to pose very tight questions. I began by trying twenty pilot interviews. These convinced me that it was premature to concentrate on a close breakdown of their social class, educational background, housing conditions, and the financial and demographic landscapes in which they took their part. All this is important, and habitual to researchers, and in time will have to come. I then discarded the pilot interviews, but decided that the first priority was to hear the man. Shaping and analysis might emerge later; but to begin with there was the difficulty of encouraging him to talk freely and to talk on his own terms rather than within the bounds of my predetermined questions. This was more awkward than I expected, and at several points I did not resist the temptation to ask leading questions. For example a direct discussion or monologue on whether they would prefer to have a son or a daughter might amount to no more than bland all-encompassing talk ('We'll have to wait and see. Either is fine.') But organized supplementary questions might reveal that they did indeed have a strong preference. I would not like to claim that what we have here is men talking impromptu, at will, and entirely as they chose. No dialogue is like that. It is always a trading relationship. Rather, I tried to loosen the constraints and, within the natural limits of advancing organized inquiry, to follow the voice. This is not an argument against much more tightly structured investigation; but yet it may be one way of making the structure so unintrusive that you attract knowledge which might otherwise be missed. The experience of fatherhood is a clear example of where such knowledge has been consistently elusive or overlooked.

This may sound not only a receptive but a passive approach. Far from it: the receptivity demanded perpetual and perceptual effort and sometimes ingenuity. As we will see, in the succeeding pages, it did not succeed every time. The main difficulty is that so very much of our information on children and on the family is ultimately derived from women. It is frequently elicited from women by women. Any survey of the literature will confirm this, and make clear why it has been so. One practical reason is that in most family studies, it is very much easier to carry surveys out during the working day, not evenings, Saturdays, Sundays or public holidays. Since only 6 per cent of mothers with children work full time, this means that it has been both easier and more usual to interview the mother at home during the day. The present inquiry was conducted almost wholly in the evenings and over weekends precisely so as to reach the men. Then for reasons of cost, custom or availability the interviewer is almost always likely to be a woman. For example, in Chapter 2 — 'Figures in a Landscape' — the periodic interviews with the families of 16,000 children were usually carried out by health visitors, all of whom were female. This is not to deny that the final interpretation of data may be made by a highly placed man — a psychologist, a doctor, an academic, a civil servant. It is simply to point to the origins of the data, which in turn explains, to a small degree, why we lack a fuller knowledge of fatherhood. Nor is it to question the validity of what one woman may recall to another. It is to point up the differences that may come if we listen to the father.

That can be difficult. Men often have a certain range of conventional responses to their place as lover, husband and father within the family and with children. They accept this as established and traditional female territory. It is not just that the man so often stands back and accepts these frontiers. It is that he frequently finds it difficult to think in any other terms but these. The old equation may be that man and work equals woman and child. The present reality may be different, with the mother working and the man unemployed and clearly emotionally committed to the child. However that is, the mismatch between the conventional response and how men feel and see is not just some technical oversight in social science: the index under M for Mother stretching out of sight, whilst the index under F for Father remains only as thick as your little finger. The male voice has not emerged strongly, partly for mundane and practical reasons, but partly because — as so many interviews here suggest — the father has not wholly discovered that voice for himself.

After the pilot stage, the procedure was to visit one hundred first-time fathers in their own homes as soon as we knew that the woman was pregnant. This discussion might be early or late, but usually took place in the first three months of pregnancy. As many of the fathers as possible were interviewed immediately after the birth. With the couples' consent, some twenty births were attended. The fathers were all then seen, again at home, in the early stages of the child's life. Other informal meetings took place all along, either to check points or quite by accident. 'Oh no, not you again,' said Peter Sykes, finding himself next to me in the shivering bus queue. What I was doing was always explained in writing, at the request of the Medical Ethics Committee, and orally stated in a standard way.

At thirty of the interviews I was accompanied by one of two colleagues, both of whom are doctors and women. They also did a dozen alone. Part of the purpose of this was to double-check on any of the medical aspects that arose. Another part was to help think out what difference it made having a woman as interviewer, and what difference it made having a man. It was very valuable and balancing to talk out the interviews together later; but broadly what occurred was that the mother immediately related to the woman doctor arriving in her home, and the father — much more slowly — related to the man. We went through parallel rather than integrated discussion. In 99 of the initial interviews, the mother was present. It was made clear at every stage that the interview was with, and about, the father. Only one woman voluntarily withdrew. The rest, certainly to begin with, still reacted as if we were inquiring about motherhood, and it was not unusual for some of the women to answer the questions directed at the man, even to the extent of explaining what he felt. The man normally accepted this, and might act only as a spectator at his own interview. It took time and effort before he spoke readily about himself. Later, when he did speak more fully, one sometimes felt the opposite dilemma: it was as if one was recording something very private.

Lastly there was the need to have some kind of demographic background against which to set these interviews, even if only to establish a rough check on the normality or otherwise of these fathers situations and place in society. This was provided by my colleague Neville Butler who was following through life 16,306 children born in the first week of April 1970. Like all other such longitudinal studies it had not been particularly designed with the father in mind. Nevertheless I was allowed to do computer runs on the data, and this gives us a set of markers to set behind our fathers. All social inquirers are familiar with the questions that lurk beneath what seems to be the most solid data: the ground is always more treacherous than it looks. But it is for this accumulation of preliminary reasons that I have attempted to enter this territory by trying to unlock, receive and then order raw experience. Perhaps we can make finer distinctions later.

The origin of this study of fathers is paradoxical. It stems directly from many years of work, either research or action, on the mother's opportunity to make choices between home or outside employment. This close concern with the captive housewife or the working woman, with playgroup, childminder, factory crèche or nursery, the claims for a family wage or experiments in changing the divisions between home and work, or the part that father or mother played in both, increasingly made me ask, 'What about the men?' Often in the discussions, arguments, projects or proposals for policy, the father was acknowledged — if at all — in little more than token or cipher fashion. And yet it was obvious that this was not so in their everyday relationship. Similarly, just as some mothers were concerned about their choices, rights and responsibilities in having a child *and* going out to work, one wondered about the fathers. Some questions were forming themselves. Did men in their turn perhaps want to spend less time as workaholics and more time with the child? Was the work-bound man sometimes set on the opposite course to the housebound woman? And might they meet somewhere in the middle? For many the question was brutally resolved by unemployment. But that seemed to leave the remainder with even more work demands on them and precisely during the costly child-rearing years. And so to thoughts about more flexible working, about role-sharing, about paternity leave, about financial benefits for the family, about preparation for parenthood.

Yet underneath was another, more important layer of experience. Did fathers feel they wanted change? Were they closing gaps between themselves and their children that had prevailed in previous generations? And could this be a change in sensibility? Men had so many ways of expressing the 'tough' sides of their nature. Were they also looking for modes of expressing the tender ones too?

I did not know. But it was clear that the old questions could hardly yield answers. The way to begin seemed to be by hearing and observing the fathers. In the following study I have tried to thread together a few of those voices, so as to give a sense of how men now move through this possible climax of experience: man into father. Doubtless every generation has to discover fatherhood afresh; but there seemed reasonable grounds for suspecting that some significant shift might just be afoot. Not sudden and dramatic, for the family is a conservative institution. But possibly nonetheless a sense of fresh movement. I can only invite you to join me in this inquiry, and reflect on what the voices are saying to us, as one looks at the explicit and implicit concepts of the new fatherhood.

'How old is a baby when its eyes open?'
'Darling, it'll be a *baby*, not a kitten.'

They spoke across me, during one of the many interviews behind this study. He handed me a mug of black coffee. I was startled, but made no comment.

He had innocence and wonder. Other fathers had a weary ring. 'Kids are just a nuisance. If I was to marry again, I wouldn't have any. My old lady wanted to have them. Only trouble was, that made me a father.'

'To start with, they killed our sex life. Then they made so much noise. And they're stupid. It's not their fault, but you've got to admit their conversation *is* boring. And they cost money. Add that lot together and what does a father get out of it? Damn all.'

Yet different fathers experienced ecstasy, a sudden sense of the primitive, a fierce hatred of any medical or bureaucratic obstacle that denied their entry into fatherhood. Like John Callaghan, ordinarily an uncommunicative and severely unsentimental dockworker:

'When he was born, the nurse — there were two of them — laid him across Anne, high up. And then one of them gave him to me. His head was moving around, real perky. I wet my finger — like this — and put it in his mouth. And then he curled his fingers round mine, really tight, really tight. I had him on this side, see? With my left hand, because it's natural isn't it? You keep your right hand free. Always has been, that's the hand you need to grab a spear or axe. I'd got my right hand up here — like this — to shield his eyes from the light. Then this nurse *snatched* him, and said "No, not like that — like this" and put him on the other side. I could have nutted her, but I just said "Well, I was shielding his eyes, like."

'It's my bloody baby, isn't it?

'And then they took Anne and the baby off for a rest, so I'm off for a few pints and tell the news. Do you know where I can buy some flowers? See, what I want is to put her on a drip feed of roses for two months. I feel so good about it. That's it — one rose a day for two months.'

John, like the others — like many men's voices in this study — may seldom have spoken so freshly and urgently in life before. Not in courtship, not at marriage, not at bereavement. Or perhaps we didn't hear. This is a book about father and child, the roots of that first relationship, and the colossal and barely discovered potential for the future child and the future parent. It is not a study of motherhood. Indeed it will in many ways partly challenge the sovereignty of that concept. It will do that by asking questions which Western men have not easily phrased, but which, as we survey the evidence, lurk in the depths of their rapidly changing experience — and may in the next accelerating decades rise to the surface with some force.

Before listening to men, I immersed myself in the known evidence as lodged in the literature. Had this indeed been a book about mother and child, I think I would have required a packed decade merely to read, ponder, organize and focus all the known work there. But to read all the central literature on fatherhood — given a first-class university archive and a plentiful supply of coffee and notepaper — should take about thirty-six working hours. The imbalance is astounding and an index of our knowledge. And if you then delve into the literature on fathers, it is overwhelmingly about deviant fathers, dead fathers, fathers in prison, lonely fathers, absent fathers or mad fathers.

The American psychologist Robert Fein once sent me a piece about how he picked his way through the specialist learned literature at Harvard, one of the world's great treasure houses. He found himself reading 'Pregnancy as a precipitant of mental illness in men' (Freeman, 1961), 'Sexually deviant behaviour in expectant fathers' (Hartman and Nicolay, 1966) or 'The husband's role in psychiatric illness associated with child bearing' (Kaplan and Blackman, 1969). And so on.

If they are not bad or mad, the ordinary fathers are frequently invisible men. I looked up one of the most distinguished series of studies that we have, mapping the actuality of children growing up, and the nature of the family in modern Britain. In the index, all I came across was 'Fathers — for fathers, see mothers'.

Where, one wonders, have all these ordinary fathers gone? And could our opening voices, like nightingales calling in the wood, lead us to new and interesting paths? As I emerged into the sunlight from the long library hours, I felt certain that we needed more evidence and discussion of fatherhood.

These men were largely the hunters in the economic jungle of the factory and the office. Babies, toddlers and young children have had their often acutely pleasurable place in the male experience but on the margins of the male life. To the child the father can be anything from remote or threatening to being almost like a visitor, a bringer of presents.

Here is Paula, one of the wives:

'My dad was just a photo on the mantelpiece. I knew the photo,

but I didn't know *him* — he worked away a lot. When he came home, I was terrified of him. He was so big! He didn't hit me or anything. Didn't have much to do with me. But I was that scared, really.'
    Or Geraldine, another wife:
    'Then Daddy would come home. He brought sweeties, he brought fun, and he brought a lovely but pretty quick bedtime. He ended the day.'
    Many of today's fathers may not wholly accept that role, either as visiting ogre ('wait till your father comes home!') or beaming bedtime giant. Or as Germaine Greer put it, father as the patriarchal unit of capitalist society which 'immobilizes the worker, keeps him vulnerable' and leaves the housebound mother as 'the dead heart of the family'.
    A strange phrase, but this exploration abounds in the unexpected and we shall see what the evidence seems to support. Before we do so, it may be worth touching on some of the questions that could emerge. There are many, and many more than I initially raise.
    Firstly, some difficulties. What is the difference — if any — between fatherhood and motherhood? Of course, some bits of that 'if any' are rapidly answered. We have just mentioned that man the hunter has traditionally had a role as the gatherer, the arch-accumulator, the one who goes out and brings in supplies. There might nowadays sometimes, in a more egalitarian society, be some quite contrary evidence, from some experiences, to which we could attend. So for the moment this is not an absolute answer but an answer to some degree: men are still the main providers, women the chief homemakers, whatever the desirability of all this. But then is it not the woman who carries the baby, bears the baby and is physically endowed to nurture it naturally? Looking through the evidence in these pages, the difficulty does not seem to be in either answering yes or no to that statement. It lies in asking the very question itself. But if one can resist that massive biological, historical and cultural pressure for an instant and black-and-white answer, the 'yes' or the 'no' may be by no means as obvious as they once seemed. That is partly why I want to explore the male experience of pregnancy, male reaction to birth and male nurturing. This is not to deny the physical facts of life, but to inquire into whether we have seen those from too narrow an angle — a kind of tunnel vision.
    Nevertheless, before the argument develops, let us record that though men may love children they can be lost for words or gestures when they seek to express their affection. Look, for a moment, at this passage from Robert Miner's novel, *Mother's Day:* feelings that many fathers here reined back, or had not discovered.

Caring for babies is a physical language. No wonder no one could tell. I caught myself in strange involuntary Mona Lisa smiles. I learned to relax a baby by caressing it. I found myself secretly touching parts of Thomas I never imagined I could.

You speak to babies with your hands, and I became fluent and uninhibited. So much touching, so much naked tactile honesty became profound relief — a living syntax of feeling always before mute. Before Thomas was born I'd worried that feelings for a male child might be ominously homosexual — that's how abstract men are brought up to be. Now as I kiss Thomas' body, nibbling and nuzzling him into shrieks of pleasured laughter, I thought only that baby skin smelled as clean as pebbles in a stream.

Yet that leads to another difficulty. We began by noting how we thought in terms of mother and child — the classic dyad. But we all know that in most families there is mother and child and father — an interlocked triad. We know more than that. A child's world and a father's world may consist of other children, grandparents, relations, friends. Both father and child will live within an interplay of close relationships. In this exploration, those other voices are sometimes brought in, simply to remind us of context. But at the same time we focus sharply on father and his new child, not because this is the central family relationship, but because we know so little about it. It is almost another country, reminding one — if you shift from mother-centred studies to this sense of men — of L. P. Hartley's phrase about the past. Suddenly you see that 'they do things differently there'.

A second question to raise is whether it always helps to think of motherhood so strongly as a biological imperative. That can have the effect of pushing the man out of the picture.

For instance, the immense, beguiling and gentle influence of Dr John Bowlby lies across the last quarter of a century of parenthood. It has filtered into popular consciousness through a multitude of other researchers, writers, educators. It then becomes what is misleadingly called 'common sense'. We will often hear it behind the voices on these pages. He, in splendid style, stops question at point-blank range: 'Mothers are specially prepared biologically. If mothers don't look after babies, then babies are not going to prosper.' The evidence ahead often questions that.

It may also question simple examples where you observe how animals behave and then apply that to people. We were, many of us, taught at school about the beehive — the queen bee, the worker bee, and the drone. And rather than being an extremely inadequate and inaccurate lesson in natural history, it imperceptibly fused into a moral fable. The animal world told us something about how man *does* behave, and how man *should* behave. All this is extremely dubious, but it is very popular and exists at many levels of sophistication. I recall being suddenly shot down in flames at an academic seminar on fatherhood by a zoologist who quoted this passage from the current issue of *Animal Behaviour*:

Among the digger wasps the male does little other than mate and drink nectar from flowers; he takes little part in the laborious life of the female. She builds an underground burrow leading to an oval chamber and fills it with grasshoppers which she has captured and paralyzed with her sting. When sufficient has been collected, she lays a single egg, and leaving the larva to hatch and feed on the paralyzed prey, she seals up the burrow and begins a new one elsewhere.

Laying the paper down, she turned away from me to the rest of the room and said, with a definitive air, 'That, *fundamentally*, is the difference between mother and father.'

But, of course, it isn't. Leaving aside the way in which comparisons between man and the animal world so often cloud our thought (and many examples emerge in the succeeding pages) as they do in popular books, the startling evolutionary distinction of man is his quality of *difference*. Fathers, unlike the digger wasp, are not eternally encased in transmitted behaviour, but are probing (often baffled, often delighted) for quite a new role. And they do it as a group, but also as individuals wondering if they should bring up their own child in what may be tomorrow's way.

We might also recall that animal research, like social science, is not at all obvious — and different answers may come if we can imagine different questions. I noted an experiment in which, for the first time, male monkeys were left to bring up their offspring, alone, during the first seven months of life. Contrary to expectation, they did not abandon them, but nurtured and played with them exactly as female monkeys do. It was just that no one had observed it this way before. As the researchers concluded in their paper, 'If as inflexible a creature as the rhesus monkey male is capable of such extensive behavioural change, it seems to augur well for *Homo sapiens*.'

Yet we can't push aside the biological imperative as easily as that. Neither history nor difference of gender can be ignored. Dr M. P. M. Richards from Cambridge offered this sense of father and childbirth:

'There is sometimes pain for the fathers. But maybe what causes the pain is the breaking of a myth on which the previous relationship was founded, a myth of shared experience with its implications, or at least hope, that all can and will be shared. Pregnancy and birth make the divide of gender and sex inescapable. It is better the myth is dispersed and that we learn to live our lives in our separateness.'

This is altogether closer to what men are — now — sometimes saying. Motherhood may be a biological imperative, and it may be that in recent times woman has found more and more ways of escaping from its limitations — by control of her own body, by claims for equality, by seeking a more equal part in the world of outside work and power. As we all know, that creates new unresolved tensions with the fact, chance, duty or delight of bearing and bringing up a child. After every exhausting climb you are met by the sight of a new range of peaks.

Nevertheless, if the modern mother is often struggling for freedoms beyond the biological imperative, consider the father. Fatherhood is a cultural invention. Otherwise, perhaps, all men would be like the digger wasp — mating and sipping nectar. It is a human construct which certainly modifies the evolutionary process. Perhaps the crucial point is that it is not evolution which makes future fatherhood. It is present fathers, such as these we meet now, who change the quality of our culture. Fatherhood is a man-made idea. As we know it, it is not about fertilizing the maximum number of females and leaving behind the maximum number of offspring. That is what nature might once have dictated. It is about love and relationship and quality in living. And perhaps what is now a male cultural imperative is establishing a new balance with the old biological imperative.

The next question we might put is whether the child 'bonds' onto its mother alone. The notion of bonding again comes from work with animals. Dr Konrad Lorenz, amongst others, demonstrated how he could get a duck or a bird to accept him as its natural parent. It was a matter of being the sole living creature in contact with the animal at some vital phase in its very early life. Perhaps looking back on his influential work, and also that of Niko Tinbergen, we should not think solely of a 'natural' parent. That might imply that ducks expect to be brought up by ducks. Whereas Lorenz demonstrates that they expect no such thing. They almost always are, but if the sequence is interrupted at the crucial point then any other duck, or any other creature (such as himself), or even a moving cardboard box, may fulfil the role of the partner in the 'bond'. That may be a protective role, it may be a nurturing role. In human terms the first may often imply the father ('I'd got my right hand up here —

like this — to shield it from the light'); and the second the mother. What we have to get away from is the apparent inevitability of the natural. For translated into human terms this has become a keystone of social medicine. The child bonds onto its natural mother. The message has been radiated by hundreds of books, by thousands of television programmes, by multitudes of medical staff. Again it looks like that ever-treacherous phrase: 'common sense'.

But this is not what research tells us about observed human behaviour, either with babies or with men. Fathers, when paid any attention to, are recorded as being absorbed and preoccupied with their new baby. And, since new perceptions sometimes need new words, this state is now sometimes described as 'engrossment'. The word is an attempt to mark that sense of the father emotionally reaching out of himself so as to encompass the new child. Such terms are temporary tools, and ultimately perhaps milestones passed in the long trek towards our own self-discovery. But for the moment it may help us to keep common sense at bay, and at least to propose that the child *could* (in ideal circumstances) bond onto the father as much as onto the mother. To propose too that there would be nothing 'unnatural' in this; though our culture, its bureaucracies, and its professions frequently stand granite-like in the way. Indeed, the child may 'bond' onto several people. In that concept the survival drive comes from the baby. But several people may 'engross' the child. There the nurturing human force comes from outside the baby.

This is altogether a much more mysterious but vastly richer way of thinking about child and adult relationships than we have known in time past. All we can cue at this point is that if we could rid ourselves of the idea and practice of the exclusive 'bond' between mother and child, and add an additional 'bond' between father and child, then we have a double engine behind that child's potentiality. Of course in theory one could go further still, but in practice — if we look at this evidence — it is not going to be at all easy to get this far.

All of us are fallible in searching for the future. But we can get better and better approximations. Dr Spock, whose healthy and benign influence did so much to give colossal numbers of modern children a less restrictive and more open upbringing than their parents, revised his basic book in old age. He noticed that his 'parents' bible' had left out fathers. And he was brought up short by reflecting in old and distinguished age on overlooked personal experience. Emerging, somewhat scathed, from the feminist wars of the sixties, he recalled what it had been like for him to be a father. 'I'd been a timid child and that's what I jumped on ferociously in my older son — something I'm heartily ashamed of now.' And, so hauntingly,

a phrase that could be the elegy of lost generations of fatherhood.
'My sons said I never hugged them.'

Next, in looking at this new terrain, I doubt if we should forget
the old-fashioned idea of social class. This is by no means a crude
matter of middle-class men being better or worse fathers than
working-class men. The difference is there, but the interplay more
subtle. Two generations back the middle-class father was frequently
an authoritarian, controlling, directing figure, perhaps anxious to
educate his daughters in a precise style, and to 'give their hand'
advantageously in marriage. That was important; but a son was even
more significant. Great care had to be and was taken over his
education, training and future career. This is significant because such
a father was not likely to see himself as nurturing, or permissive,
encouraging a child to express itself and endow it with liberties.
Suddenly, within that tiny sliver of space of but two generations,
he is altogether more uncertain about what he wants from life with
children.

The change in styles of fatherhood is coming from the middle class.
Some of the explanation may be clear. The middle-class father's
income is likely to be more certain, his working life is more likely
to involve dealing with relationships rather than things and education
and career may mean that he is accustomed to accepting experts and
professional advice. Amongst many other matters, that means he
is more open to the avalanche of baby books from Truby King to
Dr Spock, which in a society where the structure of the family has
utterly changed have replaced grandmothers as the source of such
wisdom. The working-class father may be less well read, and more
immune to these voices. The fresh news percolates through friends
and television, and mild changes in doctors' or hospitals' attitudes.
He may well have less chance of moving around the country and
so be closer to older relatives in this unique phase of his life's cycle.
On the other hand his work may offer far less chance of developing
varied *relationships* since it will usually be all about handling *things*.

But this cannot explain all, and some conundrums immediately
emerge. First of all, middle-class fathers talk much more about the
need for a close, warm, individual relationship with their child. But
they often aren't around to do it:

> *The groan of ants who undertake*
> *Gigantic loads for honour's sake*

They are commuting, pursuing their career, working late at the office,
reading the baby book on the train, but finding the baby in bed.

Working-class fathers, on the other hand, may actually be spending far more time with their child. This is because they have shorter hours of enforced work, and their unions constantly seek to reduce the time they spend on frequently unpleasant and humanly unrewarding jobs. They are also more likely to be unemployed. This takes them towards the child, whereas the middle-class father (much more likely to be a workaholic) finds a tension between his beliefs and his behaviour. But length of time spent with child and quality of time are two quite different ingredients in the mix. For the moment, we should not neglect a sense of social class as one fundamentally determining force in fatherhood. Neither should we overlook its illogicalities, and the great deal that it does not explain. Listening to what they have to say, we could attend also to that hidden voice — the expert through the media — which is so quietly but distinctly counselling them quite as much as the Oracle once did the bemused Greeks at Delphi.

Out of this then comes a whole range of possible behaviour for today's father. Never before have there been more forms of fatherhood open to him. That comes later, but I could illustrate the extremes in modern man's presence at the birth of his first child.

Here is one man in London:
'I didn't stay because I was feeling ashamed to look at her having the baby. I was scared of blood, and anyway, man should not enter a lady's room when giving birth, because man cannot do anything. Woman is different because they can wipe sweat and hold the woman's feet when the pain is great. So I left the room and started to walk up and down through the passage and the dining room, like a soldier on duty.'

Here, at the same moment, is an adviser to fathers in New York:
'Ask the nurse to snap a couple of shots of the whole family. Obstetric nurses are very good at this because they get a lot of practice.

'Delivery room photos taken by enthusiastic dads have become so common a part of the childbirth scene that one father told me the hospital had provided a mimeographed sheet of hints for camera-wielding fathers. It suggested, for instance, using a blue filter to correct for the light in the delivery room, and it had similar tips for movie making and tape recording.

'Turn the machine on when you arrive in the delivery room; you may enjoy having a recording of the whole thing — your wife's moaning and the doctor's comments *and* that powerful first scream.'

Such an astonishing arc of experience at the birth moment has probably never been there for men before. The traditional mould is cracking. And we shall watch it do so.

Or so it seems. For we still know so very little empirically about fatherhood. Graeme Russell, the Australian social scientist, despairingly surveying the scanty data, once noted that most of our knowledge seemed to come from studies on 'first-year psychology students and white Norwegian rats'. One reason for our ignorance has already emerged — our overwhelming and blinding belief in the mother-and-child relationship. But another one is more mundane. As I have mentioned, fathers are very elusive to interview, precisely because they are out at work except at the weekend and over holiday periods. That is why it is so seldom done. Most research interviews take place during the day, and consequently what one gets is the perceptions of women and not of men. You can illustrate this again and again by examining all the major surveys on family life. They report female experience.

To summarize, this is partly true of some of the evidence on which this study rests. For apart from personal experience of fatherhood, and analysis of the literature, we are here drawing on two fresh sources of data. First of all a national picture, against which we can set individual experience. The data is 11,983 fathers all of whom had a child in the first week of April 1970. This is not only a national sample, it is a sample *through time*, since all the families were interviewed again when the child was five years old. This give us a glimpse of a patterned landscape.

Secondly, we then took our hundred fathers who were having their first baby in 1980 and 1981. These are different from the national sample. Each of these first-time fathers was seen before the child was born. All were seen again at or after the birth, and every effort has been made to keep in touch with the fathers as the children grow from babyhood towards toddlerdom.

Lastly in constructing this book I have tried to keep returning to a small number with whom the reader might become more familiar as they move through the different phases of becoming a father. I could have chosen dramatically different men — one bringing up his child alone, one very conscious of his racial standing, one severe in his patriarchal authority, one idealistic in his all-embracing permissiveness. But as I said earlier, I have, as objectively as possible, tried to search out what seems to be the normal experience. I have no wish to contribute to the literature of fatherhood as abnormality, but to look towards its centrality and its sometimes frustrated and unharnessed force for creative living.

Perhaps we should lastly pick out two terms: 'gender' and 'sex' which are often used in this study. At a conversational level they may mean much the same: interchangeable currency. At a grammatical level every schoolchild is initially puzzled as to why gender in language — masculine, feminine, neuter — is not always the same as accepted sex divisions. It is not quite the same in social science, and there is no such latinate linguistic history. Yet if we distinguish the two words we have a pair of serviceable if imprecise tools — a minor way of exploring major family concepts. 'Sex' must be close to sexuality and to the traditional male and female division and relationship, whatever variants there might be. 'Gender' allows many other kinds of discussion. Two matter here. The first is the role of the man or woman. A father who rears a child alone may play, in part, the accepted mother's role. And equally so for a single mother who — to a degree — becomes a father. This shift of gender runs not only through the immediate family, but through friends and the community: neighbours can become 'aunts' and 'uncles' in extraordinary ways. The second is the cultural definition of gender: how the weight of history determines what a mother or a father is, might or should be. Looking at the styles of early fatherhood that here emerge, it is often helpful to see how both the 'old' or the 'new' father is influenced by his sex, by the role he plays, or by what was and is expected of him by others: hence the two working terms.

If we could make some progress there, then we could at last pick up the challenge that Helen Maths threw down a century ago in *Coming Thro' the Rye* — a challenge echoed by so many women and men since: 'I can't think what fathers were invented for.'

2
Figures in a Landscape

In the week which began on Sunday 5 April, 1970, 16,306 children were born in England, Wales, and Scotland.

Much else happened in that week. On the Sunday, President Nixon told Vice President Agnew not to go to the baseball match, because his casting vote was needed to appoint a controversial judge to the Supreme Court. In Britain, the Foreign Secretary, Michael Stewart, flew to Ankara with 1,200 pounds of dried soup for victims of the Turkish earthquake; and bombs exploded in the Crumlin Road, Belfast. On Monday there was rain, sleet and some snow right across the British Isles, and much of the Continent. A referee was killed by lightning after he ruled that a match should go on despite a violent thunderstorm; and Count Karl-Maria von Sprett, the German Ambassador, was murdered in Guatemala. On Tuesday the papers carried photographs of daffodils in the ruins of Lesnes Abbey at Woolwich, Huddersfield Town went to the top of the second division and a pair of ospreys returned to their traditional eyrie at Loch Garten on Speyside. Wednesday brought the coldest April night since records began, and the Brotherhood of Father Christmas and Union of Santa Claus was fined £10 for obstructing the pavement outside Selfridges in Oxford Street. Sir Adrian Boult gave a triumphal performance of the Brahms D Major symphony at the Festival Hall, and the next day brought a Conservative victory in the Greater London Council election and an Oscar for John Wayne in Hollywood. On Friday the spaceship Apollo 13 set off on course for the moon, and Paul McCartney admitted that the Beatles had broken up. The last day of the week brought the Cup Final at Wembley between Chelsea and Leeds United. For the first time ever at that stadium it ended in a draw, and the silver trophy lay unclaimed in the Royal Box.

All the kaleidoscopic quality of life not only during the first week but during the first five years of these children's lives stands out of reach in this chapter. But in the statistics, analyses and arguments that follow perhaps the reader will accept that reality is larger than record, though one tries to be as objective as one can about that part which interviews and questionnaires can capture. And though this chapter deals chiefly in numbers and statistics, nevertheless it should not be forgotten that behind every figure lies an individual child. Certainly that is how their parents, the chief source of information, always saw it.

I cannot tell the human story of over 16,000 unique and individual boys and girls. That too lies outside the scope of this book, and the spotlight here is on their fathers. But in following the data it should perhaps be remembered. It helps, just for a moment, to hear the voices of some of the mothers remembering what, to them, was their most important moment of *that* week.

'Dawn came at 4.30 on the Sunday morning. It didn't take long, it was just like a bad period pain. Somehow I knew she was going to be a boy and when she popped out I was a bit surprised — as if there'd been a mistake. But all I wanted to do was go to sleep, and let them get on with it.

'Dawn frightened me to death when I got her home. I thought I'd drop her on the floor and she'd break like a piece of jelly. And then the little perisher worried me because she wouldn't cry. I think I'd got my brother's baby at the back of my mind — that was a cot death — and it sort of shook me. So I wondered if there was anything wrong with Dawn. And a lot later it turned out there was. It was either her liver or her kidneys, and she had to go into a special unit. She's all right now — a little blonde bundle of mischief, she is.'

On the Monday it was Mrs Shapiro's turn. 'I didn't know much about it — it was a Caesar, and now I can't have any more. Not that my husband minds. You have to do it quick, that Caesar. No time for husband's permission, he was off at work. So I woke up to Lucy. She was really beautiful. Not wrinkled at all. I don't know — I'd been so distressed — she was like a shock. You see, she worked. I couldn't believe that. But all the little pieces, eyes, legs, wee-wee. Complete set, like Lego.

'I wasn't always the world's best mum. You know, cross at night when she wouldn't sleep, and then cross in the morning when she wouldn't wake up. I *hated* being mummy-cross-all-the-time. But you learn. Slowly you learn to enjoy them. Lucy is a miracle. Those first five years, we've done nothing I could tell you about. We've just had a quietly exciting life.'

Wednesday brought Jeremy's introduction to the world. 'Well, he just sort of popped out. It was a bit quick, but do you know, only a few minutes before my husband popped out too — to get the bread from the shop. I think he must have known he was coming. I didn't. But last time when we had Anthony in the hospital *he* just passed out. Search me why, but I think fathers are like that.

'Mind you, I thought it would be a girl. I think a woman always knows, and when the midwife came — I had this one at home — we played records, and she chose that Rolf Harris one, "Two little boys had two little toys".

'But it wasn't like I expected. He *was* a boy. Still, I wouldn't like these modern things when you know in advance: takes all the fun out of it. I enjoyed having Jeremy, really enjoyed it. The doctor arrived too late, but we gave him a cup of tea. I think he'd had a harder day than me, and I'd got Jeremy — but I felt he needed a bit of cheering up.'

These are only three voices. But though we are conscious of the individual nature of each child, family and experience, this survey must deal in trends over time. All the children were studied at birth, under the auspices of the National Birthday Trust Fund. A full report is to be found in the two volumes of *British Births*.* So this chapter is built on existing foundations, created and directed by Neville Butler, and allows the reader the very rare opportunity of following a large group of children and fathers through their first five years.

Not all survived. Two out of every hundred died before they were five years old. Others left the country, and this left us with 16,306 children who might be traced broadly at the moment of their entry into formal schooling when they were five years old.

This tracing began in 1974, using the National Health Service Central Register. It depends upon the co-operation of almost every area health authority and family practitioner committee in England and Wales, together with the parallel bodies in Scotland. Briefing meetings were held throughout the three countries by area nurses. From these, health visitors, all women, carried out the fieldwork. They visited every one of the five-year-olds that we could trace, and interviewed the mother. The main information sought was about the home environment and family situation; the child's illness and her or his early life experience. The health visitor then carried out developmental assessments using a specially designed booklet. To reduce bias by the interviewer, each mother was invited to

---

* Chamberlain, R., Chamberland, G., Howlett, B. C., and Claireaux, A., *British Births: Volume One — the First Week of Life* (Heinemann, London, 1975);
   Chamberlain, G., Howelitt, B. C., Masters, M., and Philip, E., *British Births: Volume Two — Obstetric Care* (Heinemann, London, 1977).

supplement these inquiries with a 'maternal self-completion questionnaire'. All three of these were filled in for 13,135 boys and girls. We were also able — from community health records — to build up a developmental history schedule for approximately 10,000 of these children. This brought together information on the child's developmental screening, on all recorded contacts with health visitors or child health clinics, together with records of any assessment for handicap or special educational placement, or any entry on risk registers at birth or during the first five years.

The next task was to try again to trace some at least of the missing children. At the age of six a new attempt was made, through the co-operation of local education authorities, who checked their school registers. The area health authorities agreed to follow up any newly identified child. This technique was surprisingly successful, and discovered 1,965 children who had eluded the first inquiry.

This chapter then is based on full information gathered under the direction of Neville Butler on 92·4 per cent of all children born in that April week. Out of 16,306 children, 426 were not traced. But the next question is what information we can quarry from this about fathers. Almost at once we hit difficulties which on the surface appear technical, but fundamentally are another example of what we have called tunnel vision — total concentration on the mother-and-child relationship. For example, the trawl of this vast surveys picks up a huge amount about women and children. But when we select our fathers we have a less complete and detailed record. This chapter is anchored in the behaviour of 11,983 of those men. Many slipped the net. And it is based on information given by the mother to a health visitor: woman to woman. So perhaps we should describe it not as men's experience of fatherhood but as women's perception of how fathers function.

That may seem a fine distinction. But it could be that it is also one of the final distinctions which we have to try to remove, as we allow and encourage fathers to speak for themselves. That noted, what we now have is quite the most reliable landscape yet sketched, against which to set this individual father or that.

I looked first at what it told us about men as workers, and what was the maximum time they conceivably have to share in the quickly passing life of a young child. Of course they had other things to do in that time — sleep, eat, be with their wife, fill in tax returns, bath, read the paper, see friends, mow the lawn, watch television, and a million other matters.

The data definitely showed that 40 per cent of them came home to a five-year-old who was already fast asleep for the evening; 11 per cent were not there at the weekends either; and 8 per cent were usually away overnight. There were other patterns too, such as those of the 20 per cent who worked shifts, and up to one man in ten was out of the action altogether, maybe because he was ill, out of the country, travelling around, in an institution or in gaol.

All these are eleven thousand personal stories. But it clearly means that half the fathers in Britain seldom see their young child, except over a busy breakfast, a complicated weekend or a welcome holiday.

A daunting thought. And yet they seem to be groping, if sometimes blindly, towards a new equilibrium between the sexes, between life domestic and life public. This is illustrated by the part they play in housework and shopping, taking children to school, playing back-stop when mother goes out to work.

In 1950, the National Survey of Health and Development, with which I correlated these present figures, told us that, according to the mothers, one third of them received some regular help from father, or 'someone else'. Poor old father, to be lumped in with someone else.

Twenty-five years later, according to the figures in front of us now, the mothers said that 36 per cent of fathers had helped with shopping or housework in the last seven days, and another 11 per cent had made a contribution alongside someone else, such as a grandparent or an older child.

This is entirely a female perception, enshrined in the research. But it does chart the fact that over that quarter of a century the proportion of men active in housework and active with their child had moved from a third to a half. That may seem modest in terms of some ideals. In human history, it is a leap.

Next it was possible to look at another great change of our time. More and more over the last decades, some mothers of young children have gone out to work. Allowing for dips as waves of unemployment cross the scene, the trend — if there were jobs — would be clearly upwards. Often it is an economic necessity for the mother to work, but often it is a search for variety and companionship — an attempt to get away from full-time motherhood. The symmetry here with fathers seeking to get *into* fatherhood makes a perfect pattern of our day.

Before marriage, roughly the same proportion of men and of women are out at work — between seven and eight out of every ten. With marriage, 95 per cent of men were then in employment, the number of women dropping a little to six out of ten. But when children come along, and man and woman turn into father and mother, then 98·9 per cent of men were at work and employed women sink to 38·7 per cent. I take these figures from the 1971 Census since that is the closest point to the national sample of fathers at which we are now looking. Later patterns of employment and unemployment will change that.

Nevertheless, four mothers out of ten is no small proportion. What do fathers do, if they have children under five? Some of the children of course are now just beginning school, or in a playgroup or nursery. And there, in effect, the teacher picks up the responsibility from the working mother.

But what is most striking, from the endless tapes which the computer prints out, is the amazing ingenuity and variety. About a third — 4,158 — of our fathers had a wife who worked: usually part-time, but sometimes full-time, when their boy or girl was just five. Between them they invented a whole shopping list of possibilities. Let me itemise it, and put a percentage in each. What I am listing is who, precisely, looked after the child during the mother's working time.

The father by himself	12·4%
The father and the school together	23·2%

This taking care of the child may be before school (if the mother is doing early morning office cleaning); it may be during the day (especially if he is a shiftworker or not employed at all); it may be after school (the latchkey hours); or it could be in the evenings (if she is perhaps a nurse or a barmaid).

Putting it all together we see that a third of fathers provide this basic back-up; and they are really the major form of care, if the mother works, with a child at this age.

The only other clear alternative is school itself, and that was true in exactly 33 per cent of these families.

After that it was a matter of making the best and most flexible arrangements you could from grandmothers and aunts, uncles and grandfathers, sisters and brothers, childminders, nurseries, friends and neighbours. Here is that last third of the shopping-around list:

An adult relative, outside school hours	6·9%
Mother working at home outside school hours	4·7%
Grandmas, grandads, uncles, aunties, cousins	4·0%
A nursery, playgroup, infant class, or some special form of schooling — for example, for a handicapped child	3·6%
Mother herself, whilst working at home	2·2%
An older brother or sister after school hours	1·9%
Mother taking the child to work outside school time	1·8%
A neighbour after school	1·4%
A childminder after school	1·1%

Mother takes child to work. Child not at school yet 1·1%
A friend or neighbour during the day   1·0%
A paid childminder. Child not at school yet   0·7%
A day nursery   0·6%
An older brother or sister, by themselves   0·4%

One meaning seems clear. A third of these fathers must expect the mother to go out to work. By the time the child reaches school age probably the teacher is educating the child during those hours. If not, then great ingenuity is used in calling on relatives, other children, nurseries, neighbours and friends.

That still means that about 1,600 of our almost 12,000 fathers *have* to be looking after the child for a significant part of time. If we then look back to our earlier discovery that 40 per cent normally came home to a sleeping child, we can see that, whatever overlap there may be, the variety of positions in which a father finds himself with a young child can be astonishing. We have the commuting father who seldom sees the toddler during the week, and the father who — within a normal marriage — *has* to play a massive part in rearing his child, because the modern mother now so frequently seeks work during the nurturing years, and maybe because he is out of employment.

These are now two normal situations. I should stress again that I have put aside all the information on single-parent fathers bringing up a child by themselves, divorced and separated fathers, and absent fathers — abroad, in hospital, in prison. All those conditions are important, but numerically they are marginal to the growing up and the fathering of most boys and girls.

Last, I'd like to consider what this information tells us about the time that fathers spend with their child, the part they can play in the rhythms of bedtime, and especially how much time they spend reading to their young child, since this is one of the clear-cut and measurable ways in which educational 'capital' in the family is bequeathed to the next generation.

But this can be deceptive terrain too. In an American study of middle-class fathers, they were asked how long each day they actively spent with their one-year-old child. The fathers estimated a depressing fifteen or twenty minutes a day: a mere sliver of time for a transient yet fundamental experience.

When a miniature microphone was unobtrusively attached to the child's shirt, the average number of *seconds* recorded each day — when father and child were making noises to each other, at each other, with each other — was 37·7.*

This present survey gives us two glimpses of intimate contact between father and child. One tells us whether the father reads to the boy or girl, and the other whether he puts the child to bed.

Again a pattern begins to unfold. Nearly 58 per cent of fathers are home at bedtime. There is no social class difference, except that unskilled workers are more likely to be home (70 per cent) than anyone else. This partly reflects fixed working hours, and a degree of unemployment. If we look at educational background it is the same story. Some 50 to 60 per cent at all levels are usually there. And 40 to 50 per cent are not.

Being at home, had they read to the child in the last week? One five-year-old in ten had been read to by *no one*. Five out of ten were read to by their fathers.

There are of course many other close forms and ceremonials of relationship between a father and a child. So this is not a judgemental statistic. It is however translucent. The better educated father is more likely to read to his child than the poorly educated one.

For fathers with no qualifications, the figure was 39 per cent; for those with a degree it was 70 per cent; for those with a teacher's qualification it was 76 per cent — almost double the figure for the unqualified. This, by any standard, is a most powerful piece of evidence. It suggests the remorseless way in which the educational inheritance is handed on. Again, we can look at the bleaker side. In homes where the father had a teaching qualification, only one child in a hundred had not been read to in that week. In homes with no formal educational background, the figure was 14 per cent at the age of five.

If we consider how much fathers of different groups, ranging from the most advantaged to the most socially disadvantaged, read to their children, the following pattern emerges.

Father reads to his child

Most advantaged	72·5%
Advantaged	60·0%
Average	45·2%
Disadvantaged	36·8%
Most disadvantaged	31·9%

It was also the case that the more children there were in the family, the less likely they were to be read to at all; or the father bowed out of this part and left it to an older child.

* Rebelsky, F., and Hanks, C., 'Father's verbal interactions with infants', *Child Development*, 1971, no. 42, pp. 63–8.

We can pursue this tantalising trail just a little further. The mother was asked who was the main person reading to the child, even if both often did so. Mothers had a clear lead here, and claimed that in two out of three households this was amongst their dominant functions. Yet — perhaps surprisingly — 21 per cent of mothers ceded this role to the man.

One historical note is worth adding. If we compare this survey result in 1975 with a previous national study in 1965, the proportion of young British children who are read to at least once weekly by their father has risen from 35 per cent to 47 per cent. Over the same period, mothers who read to the child have risen from 48 per cent to 72 per cent. Fathers are roughly ten years behind mothers in this facet of parenthood.

But it is plain that such messages as 'it is important to read to your child' are getting through as never before. I think that this and other such messages are not so much coming from their own fathers and mothers as from the voice of the 'expert' through the media. And it is the professional classes who are picking up the signals most rapidly.

So again the hunt leads us to the discovery of two chief forms of fatherhood, with a blurred area between them.

One group cannot or does not play much of a close personal role in rearing a five-year-old or keeping the day-to-day household running. They may be away at work, unlikely to help with shopping, housekeeping, taking the child to school; not there at story time or bedtime; and not backing up if the mother goes to work.

The other group has all the cluster of opposite features. They *are* getting home by bedtime, they *are* playing a substantial part in running the home, as well as working and they are probably society's major care service if the mother goes out to work.

We have also seen something of the misty regions in between. And it begins to seem as if more open discussion of the once unquestioned role of the father, more listening to what they see and feel, more readiness to help them make changes, even if modest ones, in their lifestyle and working hours, could lead to the traditional father becoming a minority figure.

Father is changing as never before. He is still inside the economic prison, often encased in attitudes from the past, and still largely ignored. Old inequalities tenaciously persist. But there is something restless about the modern father. In the past we might have said he was flexing his muscles. But perhaps what he is doing is looking into his heart.

PART TWO

Full Fathom Five

3
'Darling, I've News for You'

'She rang me up at work and said she'd come home with me because she wanted a word about something. She didn't say what. Then as we were driving back, she said, "I'm pregnant." I was so surprised I drove the car off the road. I was so excited, high. It's a strange experience. I'm going to be a father. The line isn't going to die out with me. My equipment works.'

Men meet the news in different ways. And feel and remember. But all of them hear it; none announce the headline. They may gently push the event away into a manageable middle distance, as Saul Wogan did. 'It was gradual, her being pregnant. I don't know, it came about in the normal course of events. It just gradually happened. It was just that she was getting pregnant. It was no surprise.' Or he may hold it at arm's length, like Ed Kolinski. 'We decided to have a child before it was too late. She's thirty-seven and I'm thirty-seven and we both have our careers. She made it clear *she* wanted a baby. That would be her and it. It was an Insemination Event.'

All points on the map of male experience. He may feel ecstatic, terrified, relieved, stunned, bewildered. I have found all these to be common and normal reactions, though seldom spoken about. Quite unlike the female experience where the mother naturally talks at length and in detail down the years about her pregnancy and childbirth. In this and the succeeding chapters I shall zoom in close and look at a number of men from the larger sample. I shall listen to what they say and observe what they do. The purpose is to sense the nature and the quality of the man's experience.

These fathers come from the group of one hundred, whose wives successively registered at a large modern maternity hospital which delivers over 4,000 babies a year. I simply collected the new list each week, and, with the full co-operation of the hospital and the consultant, I then saw the pregnant woman. Here I met my first and very interesting hurdle. I explained that I would like their agreement to talk to their husbands, and why. 'But what ever for — I mean I know he's the father, but where does he fit in?' I grew used to variants of that remark, or to blank stares or to even blanker incomprehension. Indeed many women, to the very end of this study, never got away from the idea that it was she to whom I wanted or should want to listen. Many was the time when the husband at last began to speak his hidden views or feelings, only to be cut off by the wife eagerly breaking in to tell me what she felt. And so the unspoken was never spoken. And on more than one occasion when the father was delayed or had to change our meeting, the mother has happily made two cups of tea and settled down to tell me his answer to all the questions I would raise. The women were able and intelligent people. I had explained myself, more than once, both in conversation and in writing. What I was so frequently meeting was not personal. It was a cultural incomprehension: the female filter.

However, all one hundred women agreed that I could see the men. I visited the men at home, on their own territory, at least once before the baby was born. With twenty fathers it was possible to see them either at the birth or immediately afterwards. All were seen again after the child returned home, and some at intervals since. Only one mother said 'Well then, I'll leave you two to it' and disappeared. Though the other ninety-nine women went away for intervals to answer telephone calls, make coffee, feed the baby, they could not pull themselves away from these interviews. At the beginning, I suggested to the first men that we meet by ourselves somewhere else, but they were clearly highly uncomfortable and I abandoned the notion. Each man was asked for his co-operation orally and in writing. This was required by the Medical Ethics Committee as a condition of the access and information I was given. When I heard of this, I sensed disaster, and imagined my fathers gently melting away like spring snowflakes. But the opposite was the case. Every single father agreed. I have never had a hundred per cent response in research, before or since, and cannot, alas, put it down to any persuasive arts of mine. On reflection, it was partly the novelty of the idea. Many men were clearly eager to talk, others curious, and even the shellbacks — whom we shall meet — later showed that, yes, they too wanted to say a lot about themselves. But I also put it down, in some measure, to the unreasonable awe in which hospitals and all who work in them can be held. People hardly knew that they could say 'no' — not to me in particular, but to very many facets of medical behaviour which I observed all around me.

The men whose voices we hear shared two more characteristics. They were all first-time fathers. Nine of the women had had babies before, but none of the men. Or so they maintained. Next, I took them off the main register of a big and busy urban hospital. This means that none of the mothers were initially seen as being complex or high-risk clients — either for social or for medical reasons. All such women were streamed off to specialist consultants. This, paradoxically, suited me. It means that we do not have adolescent boys who make a girl pregnant, or fathers who have absconded, or fathers who may be in prison. We do not have fathers who come from minority groups under great social and cultural strain. Nor fathers where there are severe medical problems, from epilepsy to mental handicap, in the family. Nor do we have fathers (the figure is less than one in three hundred) who insist on their first child being born at home.

All those are important. But this report is about the mainstream experience of the majority of men. It is about listening to an ordinary father in an advanced industrial society. From the hundred, I have drawn on a smaller group over these next pages simply to make the dynamic shifts in their feelings, before and after the baby, a degree easier to follow. Nevertheless, typical fathers are often astonishing: perhaps not, as our problem-centred literature might suggest, an endangered species, but certainly an undiscovered one.

Let me introduce you crudely to what gathering this data may be like. I called on Steve Campbell, and began by saying:

'It's very kind of you to see me, Mr Campbell. I've explained about this fatherhood research, and I wonder if we could go through a few points together and hear what you think. For example, when did you decide to have this baby?'

'Oh yeah, yeah. Is that a rugby tie you're wearing? No? You a rugby man? Yeah, yeah. Thought you were, soon as you came through that door. Er, thanks love.' (Wife serves coffee.)

'Yes, I like rugby very much. But I was wondering about your baby. . . .'

'Yeah, my first love has always been rugby. Got to be. Always played. Second row. Don't know what you think about rugby, but I'm a Scot. It's a physical contact sport with us. Come on now, we were on tour down in North Wales and there it's a different game. The ref blows for anything. You daren't *touch* anybody. You bring this bloke down hard, the ref nags at you and you just stand there amazed. Might as well be soccer.'

'Yes — though I like soccer too — but, your baby. . . .'

'Umph. It's not like that in the Welsh valleys. Punch for punch there. Come on, I was instructed, "do" the oppo hooker. So first scrum

I belted him. Next scrum — you understand rugby, yes? — well, there's no way the hooker can get me in the second row, is there? Impossible. He's hanging up there on the props. Bloody big props he had too. Then wham! clout! he thumped me. God knows how. We all ended up on the deck and somebody kicked me in the mouth. My nose — see my nose? — that was then.'

'Oh yes. Now about your baby. . . .'

'Yeah, hold on a mo'. I was bloody useless for the rest of the game. I was still angry in the showers and this little bugger from the other buggers was showering with me. Suddenly he said: "Sorry I kicked your face, boy; sorry you lost — better luck next time." And I bloody heard myself saying: "That's all right. Let's have a beer afterwards." And we did, bloody millions of them.'

'Glad it worked out. Well with the baby coming. . . .'

'Bloody great game, rugger. What were you saying?'

When I finally emerged from that first interview with Steve Campbell (but listen to him later when the baby is born) I summed it up as borderline, unusual. One type of man. He clearly knew what he was doing: fending off an intruder in his den, and saying 'Look, we shouldn't be talking about babies and nappies and all that. Let's stick to men, beer and rugger.' Some time later I felt the same as I met the fresh, autumnal night air after my initial meeting with Cheryl and Gary Butler. Gary is a small, sturdy docker. He has a silver ring in his left ear, and, though a member of no church, wears a gold crucifix, day and night, round his neck. 'Must never take it off,' he says defiantly and unasked. I talked to him about his future baby, he stripped off his shirt — all black hair, muscle and glinting cross — and swilled himself down at the kitchen sink.

Most of my carefully chosen questions were answered with grunts. Not yes, no or maybe — but just a grunt. Sometimes he would splutter a remark through the sloshing water. 'I don't agree with all these midwives and health visitors.' Cheryl was only mildly troubled about this, anxious to sit me down and make me comfortable and chat about her pregnancy.

So, feeling defeated, I sat at the kitchen table sipping coffee with Cheryl and throwing the odd remark to Gary when I could. Mostly I met with splutters and grunts. Suddenly the ritual wash was over and Gary was standing over me. Rubbing himself violently with the towel and spraying drops all over the table, the coffee, Cheryl and me.

'So what *is* a midwife, anyway? Waste of money,' he said. He knew he was to be a father. He had only the slightest idea of how a baby was born. He felt he'd *done* something to Cheryl and was frightened of what was to come.

I introduce Steve and Gary because they presented themselves as powerful, physical, aggressive males — just entering fatherhood. I was quite wrong to see them as unusual. These were both manual workers. But professional men frequently made an identical impact. They did not divert me with rugger stories or slosh in the kitchen sink. Instead they told me about the demands of their job, the difficulties of their career, the huge bills they had to meet, the journeys they had to make, the schemes they had to draft, the committees to convince, the targets to meet, the patrons they had to please. Their response to the impending birth contained quite as much machismo as Gary's grunt: the stag at bay.

There are two points that emerge, and both now become themes of this study. The first is the huge stress upon men to define their masculinity — a pressure which may be particularly intense around the birth of the first child. I hope we can so pursue this inquiry as to see how men can be helped to move from such a sharp silhouette of manhood towards a new and more generous concept of androgyny. Only the next chapters can tell whether we can begin to define that fresh dimension and realistically move towards it.

But the second point is how rarely men have the opportunity to utter their more tender feelings. In courtship, at death, here with birth — sometimes, perhaps. Certainly, the emotions are there. So too are the private words, spoken inside the head.

What is not there is the audience, the open channel. I frequently felt — and the father often said — that this was the first gut conversation that he had had about his feelings and thoughts for the child and for the mother. The woman turned inward towards herself, or to women close to her. She had a language, and a custom. The father was often trapped in mute expression. Steve, who was so keen on violent rugby, could only say what he felt about his child by his very gentleness of touch.

Nor were other men at the place of work much help. No one ordinarily had the skills or habits of the languages needed. Of course there were exceptions, who may point to a future, but men at work coped with their tumultuous feelings about becoming a father in ritual, defensive, slightly humorous, ultimately formal language. Rather like Steve being kicked in the teeth on the rugby pitch, and staggering to his feet not knowing whether he was alive or dead — yet brushing away the standard inquiry with 'I'm all right, let's get on with the game.' Early in this study it became clear that fatherhood was a tender experience with a shell around it. The space for tenderness to be expressed, to grow and to survive, was there — but so often uncultivated.

4

Decision Taker

But who decided to have the baby anyway? If I asked any couple that question directly, he or she or both in unison would almost certainly say 'It was mutual. We just decided together that the time was ripe.' What, I wonder, does 'mutual' mean, and what precisely makes the time 'ripe'? If I then approach the question indirectly, a different vista opens up. Some had stumbled unawares into childbirth. They didn't quite know how they had made love, or when she had conceived. It could have been chance, might have been carelessness — after a picnic by the river, waking at dawn as the sun slit through the bedroom curtains, groping their way into bed after the late night horror movie on television. They were the accidentals. And they were usually younger mothers (though not always — serendipity is not altogether banished by maturity): 'stardust blown from the hand of God', as the Lord Mayor of London said of an early royal pregnancy.

Then come a number of taken-aback couples whose contraceptive technique had gone awry. This is rare with women who use the pill. And occurred only once here. A normal figure would be that 3 in 1,000 women taking the pill would nevertheless conceive. It happened once also with the coil, which is 98 per cent effective; and at least three times (though I felt the figure was higher) with the sheath. Here there is an 88 per cent safety line, but it can be much lower since mistakes are all too easy in the eagerness of the moment. These dismayed fathers did not really feel the time was yet 'ripe'.

There were also fathers where there had been fertility problems. Jackie and Liam Workman had been trying for a baby for five years before she consulted the clinic, and eventually took a reluctant man along with her. He grumbled about it. 'I can't stick the standing about. I thought it was all her business, but they asked me to go too. But I just get fed up with the waiting.' Jackie, who is a blonde, wide-eyed, slow-speaking and extremely beautiful woman — she always reclined on a modern chaise-longue as I tried to talk with Liam — was delighted with the doctor. 'She was so good, the doctor. Ever so helpful. I looked forward to seeing her. You see, *his* sister can't have a baby, so maybe that's why they wanted to see him as well.'

Liam bit his lip and clenched his hands, and would say nothing in my presence. It was not at all clear that the infertility was due to him in any way and indeed neither of them had any idea of what diagnosis or treatment they had received. But after the visits to the clinic, the baby came. Not accidental, and yet not planned. It felt like a gift — but behind the gift was a father who felt the woman's taunt.

It is worth returning again to that so common remark about the time being ripe. I began to see that in many situations, such as the ones we have just observed, it was a later label for an event quite different at the time. But ripeness was there, and had two dominant elements, each different for the man and the woman. Uppermost for the woman was her age. The youngest mother here was nineteen, the oldest was thirty-two. These were overwhelmingly first-time mothers. As a matter of common sense you would expect birth rates to follow a rising and then falling curve — slowly starting in the early teens, building up to a climax in the twenties, falling in the thirties and steeply ending in the forties. That may be how it used to be, but something new has happened in our time and these couples are part of it. Instead of that arching pattern of birth, we are moving towards two dense and different moments of fertility: one minor, one major.

The teenagers have broken away. Teenage pregnancy increases and becomes a special matter in itself, rather than the beginning of that arch. The reasons may have to do with the emergence of teenagers as a separate economic and cultural clan: they have their own money, own music, own clothes, own attitudes, own self-contained style. They are a very recent creation.

They also have freedoms in sexual relationship and a degree of release from the control of the elders unknown to preceding generations. And this means babies. It also means trouble. Low-weight babies, single mothers, and often starting a first pregnancy — or the beginnings of a large family — in a bleak climate. Always there are happy exceptions, but it explains why the youngest mother here is nineteen and the youngest father is twenty-three. The teenagers with their medical and social problems were mostly moved to early specialist care out of reach of this investigation.

And the twenty-year-olds have broken away too. It is like watching a race in which the runners instead of being strung along the track are in two thick bunches — one small, and one large — with a scattering of others all along the course. The new father is slightly older each year. He does not rush into childbirth on the marriage night — unless he is very prosperous and 'breeding' an heir is the paramount claim. He pushes the moment away.

But the woman's concern is other. She may be glad to avoid teenage pregnancy, embark on a marriage, help build a home, create the start to a new career. But as the twenties move on, and thirty looms into sight, the demand to decide on the baby becomes more urgent. Who wants to enter the labour ward for the first time with a medical card describing her as 'elderly primigravida', even though a third of her fertile period may lay ahead? Besides, she may wish for other children. All that would be broadly true of the majority of mothers whom I interviewed.

Not so the men. Their vista of fertility is endless. They could be fathers at seventy. Or simply be prolific in a way no woman can be. Were they dynasts of the desert, like King Ibn Saud, of Arabia they too might imagine themselves with forty-three sons. Fathering in age and fathering in multitudes may be part of the male fantasy if not the male imagination. One herd requires only one vigorous bull.

But the normal father here is trekking in the opposite direction. He has accepted a basically female desire for one woman, one economic man. Derek Kennedy, a supermarket cashier, explained to me with firm simplicity: 'She has the baby, I pay the bills. Man and woman. That's it.' Of course many of these marriages will, in time, dissolve; and doubtless there will be other sexual or love relationships for some of these men. But what was emphatic about their view of life were the two strong pulls: the one towards home and the other towards the world of work. It was difficult for them to cope with anything else, except a sliver of social life in between.

These fathers were committed to small nest-building perhaps more than any previous generation. Another triumph for the woman. So when you explore the question — to the man — of the best time to have a first child, you come not only on the sense of time unfolding far into the future. You also enter the modern consumer society. Their surprising answers were not normally about proving the seed of their loins ('my equipment worked'), but about the need for night storage heaters, getting a car or moving to a better one, putting the garden to rights, redecorating the bedrooms, building up some squirrel money on deposit.

As we talked, one sometimes noticed signs of the relatively prosperous life of the childless couple at their last moment — the holiday photographs, the displayed *objets,* the waxed and well-washed car, the yielding wall-to-wall carpets, the comforting warmth. We may see later how the child may arrest or lower the standard of that material living. But — and the same thing ranged from professionals and managers through clerical and skilled trades to unskilled and unemployed workers — the thrust towards embourgoisement, at this phase of life, was more powerful and shared across all groups than I perhaps expected.

It was the crossing of these two drives that led to the 'right moment', and to this phenomenon of later birth. The old close link between marriage day and birth bed had, for them, been broken — and a new life space discovered. The man had a long fertile stretch, he was busy building both career and nest — each of which could go on almost endlessly. The woman had a limited fertile period, but welcomed the chance to stake out her claim in the outside world, before beginning with babies. When 'we just decided together' her finite line had crossed with his infinite one. A flashpoint. You can spotlight that because it logically means, and this is what was observed, that the stress is not on the father taking the decision, but on the mother saying: 'Now.'

No one wants to make this picture too black and white. We have noted the exceptions both outside and inside this study. And some men too had a sense of 'Time's winged chariot hurrying near'. Michael Hahn, an engineer, mused: 'Well, I'd like a boy, right? Before I'm too old. I'm thirty-one. Yes, before I'm too old to play rugger with him. Let's see — say, he's ten. Then I'm forty-one. All right, isn't it? But I don't want to leave it too late.'

Nevertheless it was the salient feeling, and it leads directly to the next layer in the question: Who decides? In the course of this research I was inevitably drawn into contact with mothers and fathers who had already one child, and were wondering about a second. June Sunderland followed up, and sent me a note: 'My husband is not keen on us having a second baby. I do not want to have a baby without his agreement but I do feel strongly that our daughter should not be an only child. Only children are never happy that they are so. While children with brothers or sisters seem to be glad they have them.

'My husband was in complete agreement over the first child. But he did not appreciate nappies, feeding and the general upheaval of our daughter at all, no matter how hard I tried to draw his interest — he had previously warned me he didn't want to know until our baby could walk, but in fact he started to be interested at nine months.

'Polly is now two and a half, and my husband and myself are

twenty-nine. I feel that if we cannot have another baby within the next year or so, the whole point will be lost. I know I shall probably bear a grudge in later years. I do realize that the baby should be loved for itself — I would certainly enjoy him/her — but would my husband? Should I just make sure we have the baby, and not tell him? I don't think he'd know what had happened. But would he love it?'

It is not easy to answer June. And there is a limit to one's role as a social investigator. But she touched a red button. Very many times I walked away from an evening interview, thinking as I navigated a criss-cross of suburban drives, avenues, views and mounts, 'Did she or didn't she?' Later I sometimes picked up traces of resentment from fathers who knew or felt that a baby had been sprung on them. But mostly — always assuming I correctly decoded the hints I was given — they had welcomed the surprising news, quite innocently.

What this illuminates is not so much the particular dilemma of this future mother or that, as her finite line crosses that of the man. It suggests something more important about the shifting foundations of fatherhood. A change has taken place in only a generation or so. Ultimate responsibility for contraception — no, more important, for conception itself — has firmly shifted away from man to woman.

Only just ahead of us in time, it was the man — maybe in the heat of action — who finally decided. He did that by withdrawing, by finally abstaining, by agreeing to follow the Byzantine temperature-and-time complexities of the rhythm method, or by irresponsibly or gaily abandoning the sheath. Not so now. The coil and pill have not only made contraception easier. They have changed the balance. The man certainly enjoys more sexual freedoms, more erotic pleasures. His ancestors must peer wistfully down the years. But he shares or surrenders the seminal power to time the arrival of that first child.

I am at some pains to emphasize the mainline experience, and the dramatic sense of change. Many exceptions must be allowed — from the new orbits of teenage birth to the possibilities of avoiding birth altogether and building the family through adoption. But, on the evidence I have, we are not only drawing the outline of the modern father, but beginning to hatch in the details. We will move closer in, but at this stage it may help to note his increasingly domestic commitment (even if, as Chapter 2 revealed, he paradoxically was often not there at all during the small child's significant living), and to sense the reason and possible consequence of our later start to building a family — on which also our ancestors (not to say the ghost of King Ibn Saud) might look with some astonishment.

The man himself, for all his public confidence, may not actually know. One expectant father put down his coffee cup, frowned into his past, and sought a clarity which eluded him. 'We both decided to have it, didn't we? We just decided together, didn't we? I don't remember how exactly it was, but we just decided. *Didn't* we?'

5

Action Man

Not that a child will make all that much difference to a man's life.
Or so thought some. 'Can't give up cricket on Saturday afternoon,'
whispered Martin with great firmness. 'Well, could you?' Or maybe
there would have to be minor readjustments to accommodate the
newcomer. 'I'm keeping an eye open for pubs with gardens, so we'll
know where to take it,' pondered Derek. If Maureen could work
out the milk-flow problem, he'd handle the beer run. And for Saul,
who amongst many other matters 'only plays squash twice a week
or so' since 'I'm a home type', then 'it won't make all that much
difference, if any. We can take the baby to squash in the car, and
Liz can park it in the bar. Hey! that rhymes. No, it'll be all right,
all that. No trouble.'

Other fathers were inventive in imagination: the new child added
to the landscape but did not inconveniently alter it. 'A friend of June's
has a good idea. She's trying to change the baby's day so that it's
awake when he comes home. We're thinking of doing that — sort
of keeping it in bed longer so that it's down here when I come in.
We can do that about everything and just carry on as normal. It's
just getting the principle right, isn't it?'

Just under a third of the fathers entered pregnancy with this
innocent sense of minor disturbance. Another third or more were
natural Fabians. Like the Roman general Fabius Maximus Cunctator,
they did not anticipate sudden victory or blinding defeat, red
revolution or cataclysm. They felt it prudent to pursue that policy
which is based on the inevitability of gradualness. So they put
themselves on a course, and degree by degree reduced their social
life a little.

'We keep trying to cut down on social life. I tell her, we've _got_
to get used to that. But then she goes mad, and says "This might

be the last time" and off we are in a whirl after work every night
again. But I think we've *got* to cut down, train ourselves, that's
discipline. Some time. But you tell her!' Or, as Cameron says, very
much playing it cool to me, 'I've got to scale it down, man. Yeah,
we've got to scale it down. Get the chicky little nest all ready, all
right?' Cross-legged on the floor, Marilyn puckers and then smiles
a slightly dubious but strongly hopeful 'Yes'.

Those were these two salient types of father — the innocent and
the Fabian. Or so they presented themselves, for men wear many
masks, in public and in intimate situations. The last and missing part
of the triad split sharply into two contrary responses. Some men
resented the heralded arrival. 'I know what it will be. I can imagine
coming home after a hard day's work to a hard day's night. No,
quite frankly, I don't look forward to it. *She* does.' Perhaps more
felt this than dared to say so. He took down one of his wife's books
and pointed out a quotation to me: 'A baby is nature's answer to
the silicon chip — a small component that governs the activity of
a large machine.' Whether that is true or not, underneath, the most
off-hand men were thinking. Usually a private, sometimes
desperately subterranean thinking.

But the last and perhaps ultimately the most significant minority
of future fathers utterly welcomed not only the baby but the
disruption of their economic and social lives. It was not — along
simple, traditional lines — that they wanted to drop out from a
masculine and public life into a feminine and domestic one. The
reality was more criss-crossed than that. But there was, if only half-
apprehended, a reaching for a whole instead of a stylized life. And
once again the quest for tenderness. To these fathers we will return.

For, after the shock waves had slowly rippled themselves out, most
men now seemed to move through three broad phases. These almost
matched the trimesters of the woman's pregnancy. Not quite. There
were blurred edges and many exceptions, but the first stage was one
of action. After that came one of doubt. Thirdly an experience which
I can't yet describe, but one which has a quality of rhapsody about
it. That may not be the right word: let's wait.

To begin with came action. I don't mean that the man *did* anything
at all, but that he thought in terms of action. At first his words were
largely about 'how I feel'. Now they switched to 'What shall I do?'
— plans, arrangements, decisions. After those first shock waves
ebbed away, he thought about the likely change to come in his daily
style of life. That was the beginning of action thinking.

Now came the looming question of work. And along with the child
and the mother this perhaps comes to be the strongest force to the
man in this study. At first it looks easy. Nelson Owen simply says,

'No problem. I'll probably take a couple of days off. The foreman is OK. Unpaid leave of absence. Pam will be all right.' Adrian spotlights the question and solves it even more easily. 'I've arranged about the Saturday when the baby's due. We're all free then. We don't have any special time off for having a baby.'

This expectation (we will later meet the realities) of 48 hours off to welcome your baby was the norm amongst the manual workers; especially those in small enterprises or in casual or non-union employment. There was a sharp leap in expectation from two days to two weeks with skilled factory workers, clerical and lower managerial ones. So Liam Workman, who had the fertility dilemma, had no problem either. 'I'll just put in for two weeks. That's normal. I look after the shift on the acid plant. If you tell them soon enough, they've got time to sort it out and fix up cover for me.' But Derek, the cashier, who also thought that two weeks off work was 'about right', couldn't claim it so easily as paid leave. 'Two weeks, I should say. There won't be no bother at all. The doctor tells her the dates. I tell the boss I want two weeks of my holiday then. The office fills in my holiday chart — red blocks. I get a baby and lose a holiday. Not that I think we'll be thinking about holidays after this.'

If we listen to the professional and managerial groups we might expect a more generous expectation of time with wife and newborn baby. Maybe a month? But not at all. 'It's awkward,' said Trevor. 'I'll slip away as much as I can. Lengthen weekends. Avoid trips away — that sort of thing. But I just can't be out of the office, or out of action, not that long. There's a limit. A pretty short one with us in these times.' The time squeeze also gripped the self-employed: 'I can't really take *any* time off. I'll take 48 hours when Sue goes into labour, but there are only *two* of us. That's all. After that I'm doubtful if I can manage anything. Coming home will be like a cold bath for Sue.'

The only fathers who could hope to give more time (although others may later triumph against the odds) were the unemployed and those with very flexible work — especially men in schools, colleges, polytechnics, universities. This part of the micro-study vividly confirmed the broad pattern of the national inquiry into 12,000 fathers — and it helped us understand why.

It is useful, at this stage — because larger arguments will move from it — to record how much essentially *working time* these fathers-to-be foresaw that they must take off in order to be present with mother and child at and around the birth.

Later we shall compare this with what actually happened. The most favourably placed at this stage are men with flexible working time like Anthony Moreton, who is an itinerant thatcher, or Graham

*Amount of working time that 100 future fathers
planned to take off at the birth of their first child*

No time at all	9	all were self-employed or enjoyed short or flexible working patterns
Two days	12	chiefly wage-tied manual workers
About a week	26	dominantly blue-collar workers drawing on holiday time
About ten days	3	as above
About a fortnight	21	mostly managerial or clerical workers
Up to three weeks	4	as above
A month	1	an executive taking his holiday
Unemployed	7	infinite time, but major financial pressures
Not yet decided	17	a social scattering of fathers who had not yet seen the dilemma

Goulding, who is a computer consultant. Or much more commonly, men working in education who, at least for a while, can cram their work into a small time space. But the two key elements are as clear in the numbers as they are in the voices. One is social class. Manual workers planned to take less time off. It was a matter not of discussing it with wife or doctor, but of placating the foreman. Holiday time could be used, but there was always the risk of jeopardizing your job, or being moved in absence to a more unpleasing or less rewarding one. Managerial workers, who enjoyed five or six weeks annual leave, could gamble a fortnight so far ahead with ease. The second element was cultural perception of the mother's need and the father's role. Some men tried very much harder than others, if not always with success, to make this family time. This was not altogether a matter of class. Or, at least, men to whom this was a blind spot were quite as likely to be rolled-umbrella London commuters as the tattooed dockworker who showered Cheryl and me with his kitchen sink rinse.

Nevertheless, eighty-three of the fathers, for whatever reason, had very quickly taken two decisions — one about the change in lifestyle, one about time off work. But it was the third decision that gave more trouble now: What should the man actually do when the woman went into labour? And when would that actually be? As we have heard, some — and this is just as true of first-time mothers — actually believed at this stage that the doctor could just about spot the very day ('Well on that Sunday, I'll . . .'). Others were like tom-cats on a hot tin roof, and immediately created an emergency communication system. Michael began to ring his wife exactly at noon for a state-of-play report. He kept that up for over six months until the birth came. It was rather like telephoning for the latest score in the test match. No sooner had I thought that, than I saw Eamonn, a cricketer, who always rang in the tea interval. 'He never used to ring me before or during a match, did you darling?' She was very pleased and showed it. Cricket widow transformed into wonder woman. In his eyes, one who might erupt into birth at any moment. Saul Wogan, I was not surprised to see, had neatly packed a suitcase for his wife six months before the day. Fresh fluoride toothpaste, fancy-wrapped herbal soap, thick romantic novelette, monogrammed copper-coloured towel, a new white nightdress, and no doubt an intimate card in the bowels of the leather case. From so precise and rigid a man, it was again a signal. A beautiful and a practical one.

Other men worried about snow-drifts, flat batteries or traffic jams. 'What if it happened in the rush hour? Would I just put headlights on, pap-pap-pap, and drive through the lot? Must happen. If the cops stop you, do they let you through? My god, hope it isn't like that. Rather phone for an ambulance. But I'd have to do it, get her there on time. Got to.' Almost the vision of a city cowboy driving hell for leather to that far-off hospital. At this moment, only a minority of first-time fathers had a realistic idea of the early symptoms of labour and the time available. If anything, they had an imagining of pace, panic, frenetic action, blood, emergency. Compare this with the later reality. In it all they were wanting a plan of action, a blueprint which told them not what to feel, but what to do. That meant Saul's suitcase, necessary record cards, telephone, transport, coins in the pocket, iron rations, contacting relatives — and above all what to do to help her at the onset of birth. Such information was wholly absent. Even their very presence was, to them, dubious. 'Are husbands expected to be *there*?' Andy very hesitatingly asked, and his wife tensed herself for the answer she desired.

6

Doubtful Days

'At first it was all clear. We were going to have a baby. But now it's all cloudy. I don't know what I'll do, or if I'll be any use. I've never changed a nappy. I was amazed when she told me how big they are when born. I don't know at all. I've always avoided handling a baby, in case I dropped it. Like I said, it's all cloudy now. Perhaps after it's born — hope so anyway — it'll come all clear again.'

After those first swift male reactions — life style, pulling out of work, B-day itself — the seeds of doubt began to settle. Some were about a man's image as he entered a dark, female and unknown world. Some were straightforward doubts about cash. How was all this creation of a family life to be paid for? Most clear of all was the father's lack of knowledge ('Darling, it'll be a baby not a kitten'), and his difficulty in getting access to the data that he now required. What happens, what can I do to help? Lastly, all the fathers began to see ahead of them not only a line cutting through future time ('my equipment works'), but the dependent child — 'that powerful first scream'. And they wondered, very much, whether they had fathered a daughter or a son.

Naturally there were many other doubts. They settled on the margins of the male mind like a strange flock of black crows. All men saw them out of the corner of the eye. 'At first it was great,' said Anthony, the thatcher, using almost exactly the same phrase with which Michael opened this chapter. 'We'd been trying for years, it seemed, well months probably. She wanted a girl, so we'd talk in bed about names. Sophie, we settled on for that. But I'm sticking out for a boy. I've got that *gut* feeling that it's certain to be a boy. But now I don't know. I don't just think like that. I notice handicapped kids. We have a child in the village, and you see them on telly and in papers and I think "What if it should happen to us?"

It would still be me, wouldn't it? Part of me, and you can't — well, you can't tell. Well maybe they tell you in advance. It's all electronic now or acupuncture or something. Maybe they give you warning. The red light. We'll just have to see. That's what's on my mind. Handicap. Not that I say anything to Betty, but when I'm thatching, on the roof maybe, trimming the reeds, the edges, well, it kind of creeps into my mind.'

Let me now take the first four dubious areas. That fear of handicap comes to the surface again later. But one of those four shadowy places was the man's sense of what essentially was masculinity.

Clearly, to him, it was winning a woman. Certainly, then, it was usually some success in that economic jungle. Now it was fathering a child. Yet the prospect of birth brought it under challenge. 'Expect I'll need more help than my wife,' murmured Michael. And Ray recalled his first, tentative visit to the hospital with his shy wife when the tall, gaunt Scottish sister addressed him like the company sergeant-major on that last parade ground: 'I hope you don't mind the sight of blood. If you faint when she has the baby, you'll just have to lie on the floor, and we'll step over you — because we'll be too busy looking after *her*.' He ruminated afterwards over instant coffee. Clare awkwardly soothed him. 'Like I should scoot or be King Kong. It wasn't me who was saying that — it was them.' Even if the father doesn't feel that he is the tough, strong and silent male, nevertheless he can meet these fierce cultural and professional pressures that force him back into that role.

But the worry that now came snapping at the man's heels was money. Before the announcement of pregnancy, the man and the woman had often reached a standard of living from which, they judged, a family could be launched into a better future. There were accidents, and exceptions, and different couples had utterly unequal views about the desirable nest. All the same, not only mothers but also most fathers were concerned about this — and would usually demonstrate it in terms of cost or consumer goods possessed. 'We worked real hard to build up the stake for this mortgage. Then we have to have a car. You have to with a baby, don't you? Or you're stuck.'

All the same the cost of the future child was hidden in the mists. The woman did not worry unduly. She was having the baby: enough is enough. But the man had doubts. These couples had largely come to expect a gradually rising standard of living. Some were knocked back by unemployment, inflation, personal misfortune. But, whatever their social position, they were young, fundamentally optimistic, gathering in goods — and then going for baby number one. None of the men had realistically foreseen the financial cost.

Perhaps they should not try to do so. Nevertheless, I invited twenty fathers to cost out the exercise with me. They very much enjoyed the problem and felt on home territory. The question was: what do you estimate the real financial cost will be of your first child from birth until the official school leaving and marriage age of sixteen? This may seem cold-blooded. But it was tackled by the fathers with relish: a real question, bubbling inside them, which they were curious and relieved to try working out. No one refused. No one said a baby is priceless and so end-stopped the question.

I had a series of estimates in my hand. There has been some, if not enough inquiry into this costing, and allowing a reasonable margin of error I felt I broadly knew where I was. If I had set up this exercise about a new car and arrangements with a finance house, or a new house and the agreement with the building society, they would almost all have hit the bull's eye. When it came to money, they knew what was what.

When it came to the cost of a child, they knew nothing. Not one single father got near the probable expense. The gap is so consistent that it provokes further questions. The first baby is the most expensive investment that any man will normally make. If we rule out lucky factors or the super-rich, and take a standard father at any social level — *this* will become his prime financial cost. In the bourgeoisie, the only runner-up is the house itself.

So why do fathers, who pride themselves so frequently on their knowledge of the public domain, get the most crucial sum of their lives all wrong? Like later divorce, this could be the arithmetic of disaster. Bits of the answer to this curious mismatch begin to emerge from these surveys. Fathers, as I met them, are on the whole generous people who instinctively place the baby outside the accounting book. That may do them great credit, but it even more strongly commits them as providers, and ultimately heightens their tense relationship between work and home during the child-rearing years. Next, very few men indeed appreciated that the significant item in the cost of a first child was the loss of the woman's earnings. Later children cost less. But for the woman to move out of work is to place the full emphasis on the man's power to earn. Lastly, the considerable recurrent items of expenditure — from birthday treats to clothes, room and holidays — which all lay ahead were mostly invisible to him. It is as if there was a feminine screen. Or a male blindness.

Of course there was not. What we are seeing is the mixture that makes modern man: touches of chivalry, elements of arrogance, areas of innocence. Yet altogether here was part of that dynamic in which he belonged, the economic world of work, even at the very moment when he reached out towards the world of which his child would so soon become the centre.

The point of the crude, eagerly accepted financial challenge proved to be this. Almost all of these fathers were making the major financial commitment of their lives. Naturally it was inextricably involved with marriage, future children, property, income. Nevertheless it was intellectually detachable. Almost none of them perceived it like that. None at all came within guessing range of the personal money cost to them. And yet this was their natural field, their very line of operation. Why they got the simple sum so absurdly wrong was not because they lacked expertise, not because they had no interest. Both they enjoyed in abundance. It had to do with the intimate masculine perception — even the crucial cash nexus — of the feminine. And, as we move towards, if not a definition, a fuller understanding of fatherhood, these honest doubtings might become part of our certainties.

Rowntree, almost a century ago, pointed out the likely social cycle of a wage-earning or salaried family if they, fortune or the state did not change it. A couple marries, both move into employment, they can accumulate assets — such as a house, furnishings, a car. Or they have leisure money — it may go on sport, hobbies, evenings out, holidays. Then they have a child. One of them, almost always the woman, is no longer earning income. Simultaneously there is a new cost. There may be a readiness to have children close together, and this brief spacing means that costs increase (though not so dramatically as with the first child) and that the woman may remain out of paid work. There comes the two-decade task of bringing up children, and then, almost as suddenly, a plethora of adolescent income earners. They, too, marry and move towards childbirth, whilst the original couple move towards retirement, and once again a declining income.

Most of these fathers were clearly placed within that cycle. Few sensed it early. 'Money's the worry,' said Robin. 'Not just the two of us any more. It all depends on me.'

If men felt doubts about their own image, and if they now began to wonder about money — either money to meet basic bills or those loose pounds to finger in the pocket which funded their pleasure — they were next to sense their ignorance of birth itself. In theory, all could have attended parenthood classes. In reality, nine did so, and ninety-one did not. Some, like Robin, knew all about their existence but shied away: 'I'd feel alone — an outsider. All those women. I'd be an alien. Those women presenting it all, as if the father was there on sufferance. As if they were thinking "Well, suppose he does have something to do with it." '

The fathers who did attend classes — they were all more highly educated or enjoyed flexitime jobs — broadly confirmed Robin's feeling. 'I went to the first one. Too concentrated. Too much rammed into me. Maybe the women knew a lot more, maybe the medicos were showing off. But just that first class ought to have been three or four for me — more leisurely pace — I don't know. I felt like little-boy-at-the-bottom-of-the-class. I went to the others, just to support her. But honestly I felt suffocated with women and medicos. Learned much more from a television programme we saw, and from pieces in one of the magazines she gets down at the supermarket.'

Derek Kennedy also dutifully tried parentcraft classes. He too met the ritual challenge of 'We'll have no time to attend to you. We'll just step over you and get on with it.' He had never physically handled a baby, and, hungry for information, felt that 'TV really tells it to you. All I know has come off that screen, there in the corner.'

So why did most of the fathers not even go as far as this? Some like Adam Smith certainly felt excluded. 'I feel kept out of it. Never seen the doctor. All the news comes through *her*. She's good at telling me, very good. She's a marvel. But I wouldn't mind someone telling *me*. I am the father, aren't I?' Bob Young too champed at the bit: 'No, I've never been to the hospital or these classes. I wait till Liz comes back, and then I want all the news. Really drain you dry, don't I, Liz?'

Others, like Jack Diamond, saw it as a division of duties. 'Didn't go to any classes. That's Brenda's job. There's no need. Seen it all on TV and so on.' Or like Pete reduced it to a norm. 'No. I'm not going to any classes. Well, it's common sense, isn't it? My sister-in-law gave us a Mothercare book at Christmas, and I've looked at that, a bit. What could I do anyway?' Or Gary, who once spluttered water over Cheryl and myself. 'Nothing for a bloke to do. Not till the kid's older. No I won't go. Take it as it comes, like.'

Liam was also not going to attend classes. And never did. But he also worried in case Jacky spent money on acquiring such useless knowledge. 'Don't rush off buying books,' he told her as we all three sipped our tea. 'If you need 'em, there's always the public library.'

Very shortly, most of these fathers are to behave, quite dramatically, in a far different way. Why, in these vital days, did they resist critical and practical knowledge about the baby to be born? Not that they were alone. Many mothers (though far less so than fathers) also pulled the shutters down. 'What can they tell me?' said a raven-haired girl of twenty-two, who clearly had no idea about motherhood at all. 'It's just common sense.' I heard that defensive phrase so often that it began to grate. Or, at least, winked at me like an early warning signal.

So the men were not alone in their resistance, nor in their shielded doubts. Yet we can analyse the masculine stance. If it is a good idea for men to be knowledgeable, practical and sharing partners in the birth and rearing of a child, then we have to listen to their attitude and think of the effective flow of information. Their attitude was often one of ignorance and fear.

They frequently commanded the most amazing technical knowledge — from advanced transport systems to the microchip revolution — but when it came to birth their mind might possess no more than a sketch map. Their sense of the women was intensely erotic. ('Sometimes it gives me a thick 'un just to look at her,' Liam confided.) But with woman as the bearer of the child they were frequently lost. The knowledge they needed could have been given to them in some form a long way back: part of their basic sense of human relationship. Had they been offered some education for future parenthood during their schooldays, then antenatal classes which included men would be less threatening, more welcome, a topping-up exercise just when you needed it.

From that lack of knowledge, fear stemmed. More than half these fathers were in the same mental state about childbirth as was common amongst women — half a century back. They were fighting off a biblical sense of blood, pain and guilt. 'I'm not keen on blood,' said Sandy, unasked. 'I'm not a coward. Never have been. But I really hope I won't be allowed in the labour ward. It's her blood, you see. Not like a bottle-fight outside the pub. I don't know, but it's different. Her blood.'

That was enough to keep those who most needed the help away from antenatal classes. But it is also fair to say that there were practical reasons which excluded them or made them feel uncomfortable. The times of meeting were often based on the rhythms of the woman's day. I went to classes at 10 a.m. in the morning or at 2 p.m. in the afternoon and listened to formal regrets about the absence of men. I was often all alone — and not even consort to a pregnant lady. Clearly the men could not possibly be there. They were at the other pole — work. The unreality was curious. Everyone else knew where the men not only were but had to be. Why then call the meeting at this time, why express such forlorn words for our missing partner?

The men who did turn up often clearly felt awkward ('an alien'). After dozens of such meetings, I walked home under bright Orion in the black sky, trying to analyse why they did not work. Many men were wanting simple, accurate, reassuring and shared knowledge — at first hand. But they had met two mysteries. First of all, the mystery of medicine. I listened to so many different doctors or paramedical personnel who basically avoided communication whilst endlessly talking. What they had to tell was not complex. But instead of building simple bridges to the audience they built castellated walls around their profession. I saw this so very often that I could not put it down to a few individuals or so: it was a phenomenon. It frequently looked to me, sitting in the plastic-chaired back row, as if the prestige of medicine was invariably related to its failure to function as even a primitive communicator.

But the women too were an excluding force. It is a theme which sounds again at moments in this study. Often they seemed not to want the father inside this centre of knowledge. Instead, they liked to take the message intimately home to him. 'I really like it when Anne's been there. I squeeze out every drop, don't I, darling? She gets the gen, and lets me know, like, so we've got the picture — the baby's going to be OK. Yeah, Anne's really good, aren't you darling, at putting me in the picture?'

Men are such powerful animals. Maybe both medico and mother sensed that if they once invaded this private terrain of birth — feminine and professional as it is — they might not, like me the observer, be so easily confined to those back-row seats.

Once again comes, from the mists, this message of men on the move, not always easy to decode. 'My man', as Carmen half said, half hummed, 'he just makes this great choice of notes. New ones all the time. Just when you think you know what he thinks, he thinks something else.'

7

Couvade

Now the fathers entered the couvade. Or at least some of them did. The male couvade is a puzzling phenomenon of which we know little. The word was coined in 1865 by an anthropologist, Sir Edward Taylor. It has been widely used since in reports of tribal life — where the father takes to his bed, or wears women's clothes or is delivered of a stone or a doll, after imitating the pangs of labour. There are scores of variations, usually located in South American, Polynesian, African or Indian life — the prime areas where the founding generations of anthropologists did their fieldwork. It is usually observed close to the onset of labour and it is argued either that it is a ceremony to ward away evil spirits from child and mother, or a public declaration of paternity and responsibility. In societies where man was coping with frequent death in labour, and huge mortality rates amongst the newborn, this may well be so.

But the Western father today is a quite new animal. As we see, he worries about his child being born with a handicap, but the thought of death at birth — once a common feature of human experience — hardly flits across his mind. Indeed the fathers here, even though none of the womenfolk had been medically classified as at risk, were nonetheless too optimistic about the difficulties of birth and its outcome. Such is the revolution in expectations.

The couvade that we observe in them is not at all the same or even related to what the anthropologists have recorded. The couvade may be a very recent cultural change in the father as, in the small and separate modern family, he has closed the gaps between himself and the woman and his child. It is as well to be clear about this shift in meaning because couvade (from the French 'couver' — to brood) is such a very useful term.

There was a whole range of brooding signals from many of these fathers. We have of course to agree on the signals before we can say what proportion of fathers are affected, and here one might take a different and a wider view than we find in the scanty literature on the subject. I began to pick up the signals most consistently not at the onset of labour (as with tribal societies) nor yet at the announcement of pregnancy. They came after the man had taken the force of the news, after he had worked his way a little through some of his succeeding doubts. The couvade signals clustered in what was, for the woman, the second trimester of her pregnancy.

I started to group them under headings. For example, a heightened interest in pets. The most dramatic was Saul Wogan. His mother had given them the cot for the coming baby. He himself had bought a dog. He was continually kissing it on the nose, nursing it, holding it close and staring into its eyes. He spoke to it in baby talk, and kept telling it 'You're *such* a baby.' It slept in mother's cot and he automatically covered it with a blanket whilst we were talking. Of course many men are fond of dogs, but with Saul I classified that as brooding, because he was so physically intense with the creature, handled it like a baby, spoke to it like one (none of your 'Kill, kill, kill' here), had acquired it at this anticipatory moment, and gave the dog the cot. It all looked most unhygienic and I can't imagine what mother thought. The pet was an embodiment of the baby still hidden from him inside the womb.

Glynn Meredith already had a dog. A couple of months after his wife's pregnancy was known, he bought another, and was intensely interested in them. He now treated the older dog as if it too were a puppy. He had emotionally reduced its age. The whole arrangement looked very impractical and the last thing that particular family needed, with a baby in sight, were two bounding, demanding and expensive dogs. Others behaved similarly with cats, cradling them and cosseting them rather than leaving them to catch mice. It was sometimes the same with smaller creatures, pet budgerigars or even neon-lit tanks of fish. There was much chat about what 'company' the pet would be for the baby, however unlikely that seemed, and 'Won't you wonder what's happened when you don't get all this attention any more?' This last and frequent remark surely shows a degree of self-perception that the man had indeed entered a couvade.

A different signal came from Bob Madge. He had no time for pets. But he became something of a fitness fanatic. He joined a health club where he could exercise on the machines, take a sauna and sip carrot juice. He weighed and monitored his own body quite as much as his pregnant wife and quite casually said 'I've got to get fit for that baby.' It was an identical parallel to his wife's preparation for birth, and there was also the same sense of a concluding date. A slightly different signal came from men who distinctly began to take more care of their own safety, perhaps by wearing a hard hat on the building site or driving more carefully home. Of course this had an element of new responsibility about it, and the more thoughtful driving was sometimes freshly protective to the woman if she was a passenger in the car. All the same, it also had an inward-looking quality, very similar to the woman's frequent self-absorption with her own body.

But the classic signals of the couvade were physical and this is how we sometimes define it, though it could be too narrow a definition. Robin Carter saw his own couvade quite clearly. 'I've put on three quarters of a stone since Sally got pregnant. I'm keeping up with her all right.' You could say that he was simply eating more to compensate for Sally's shift of attention from him to the child. But that clearly isn't the whole truth: like some other men he had a wry physical sense of looking like a pregnant father. 'I'm one of the pregnant people', said Frank, who had also gained weight.

The two most dramatic examples were Ray Kennedy, a car salesman, and Tim Osborn, a market gardener. Both had visited their doctor complaining of mysterious pains in the abdomen. Neither puzzled doctor could find anything at all wrong. Other symptoms reported by men were wind, constipation, backache, 'a feeling of fullness in my stomach', strong changes of taste in their food and drink, and new broken sleep patterns.

If we broadly accept these as a cluster of couvade signals, then how many men does it affect? It is extremely difficult to know. Not only can such signals be ambiguous or also have other explanations, but many men don't spontaneously volunteer the information, since they don't entertain the concept itself. Similarly the interviewer's eye for this detail only becomes keener as the work moves on. The 'baby' function of pets, for example, simply did not occur to me until I hit a very striking and overt case. However, other researchers do also report this finding. Robert Rein, in an American study, took a group of thirty middle-income couples who attended childbirth education classes. Two of the men saw themselves as having couvade symptoms, and others had them unawares. Other American research suggests six or seven out of every ten men.

In our present hundred fathers, seven saw themselves as being in the couvade and thirty-four appeared to be. I am inclined to think that the actual figure is somewhat higher, and perhaps we could reasonably proceed on the assumption that one man in two now goes through such an experience, and one man in two does not. As to whether this is a changing phenomenon, we have no evidence. But within the context of other matters reported in this study I tend to think that it is probably increasing and is linked to the emergence of the new nurturing role with many men.

Now too the men became more absorbed in the shape of the woman's swelling belly. Ben Sutherland didn't like it, and in a pained aside muttered confidentially (Lucy was making coffee in the kitchen), 'I was surprised when the *lump* came.' Others like Saul were not sure what they *ought* to feel. 'Some men are turned on, some find it disgusting,' he mused. 'I suppose it'll go in time,' he murmured hopefully, and then, feeling his way around a new and perplexing sensation, 'I'm indifferent. Is that the right word?' It wasn't. Like some others he felt a degree of bewilderment as the experience unfolded. Doctors were beginning to counsel an armistice in sexual relations. A handful of men moved into separate bedrooms. Most, to whom pregnant women, until this phase, had been mostly invisible, now found they flashed into focus, in shops, along the streets, on buses, and occasionally at work. They mentioned it; sometimes they compared shape and size and style. More often than not they had, to my visiting eyes, an exaggerated sense of the woman's burgeoning size. As Jack O'Brien said, 'It's not a bun in the oven she's got. We've got a bloody Christmas turkey.' Notice that 'we'.

Next came the search to reach the life inside the woman: the new element in the emerging triad. Few of them saw the doctor with their wives, and of those who did only one was handed a stethoscope to listen to the heartbeat. Yet they so often struggled to make the contact and make the bond. They felt the tiny but dramatic rhythms of the moving baby in bed, or perching on the edge of the bath wondered if that spasm could really be a son's elbow or a daughter's foot. Yet they were wary. Robin told me how he loved to stroke his wife's belly, but in the very finest, fingertip gentle way lest he 'poked its eyes out'. Some had visited the hospital, and though denied the elementary reassurance of the stethoscope — which is simply one of the spanners of medicine — found some hope of basic information in the new technology, even if that still divided the sexes. Liam made his point: 'I liked seeing the instruments. I enjoy instruments. But instruments are my job, like. Unfortunately the sister didn't seem to understand them. But instruments are my job, like, at the acid factory, and I'd really like to know what's going on there, inside her.'

So, finding themselves on the wrong side of a cultural and professional divide, they turned to homely methods. Almost all tried to listen to the foetal heartbeat. Some picked it up, but it was like tuning into a far-away radio station. 'It's like listening to a watch . . . ticker, ticker, ticker, ticker, ticker . . . real fast,' said Derek Kennedy, after many attempts. Adam Smith was more dubious about his attempts. 'I've tried to hear the heartbeat. I *think* I heard it, but if I did it was very faint. I wasn't allowed to see the scan or anything like that. *She* told me all about it.' Robin was certain that he failed: 'First time it kicked, I put my head down and tried to listen to its heartbeat. Didn't hear a thing. All I got was a kick in the ear.' Ben Sutherland was certain he had succeeded: 'You *can* hear its heartbeat. I put my ear down and it was there all right.' And Bob Young emerged as the most determined of this frustrated band. 'The doctor didn't give me a stethoscope to listen. But I've been trying with the beer glass on Liz's belly, haven't I love? In fact I use a set of five. But it's very difficult.' Alternative technology could go no further.

These men were searching for a bond with the unborn, waiting for a cue to come on stage as 'the father', even to enfolding the baby imaginatively inside themselves. Adam said, to the clear amazement of his wife, 'The time I like best is when she's fast asleep. She sleeps with her stomach to my back. It's more comfortable that way, isn't it? And sometimes I've woken up in the middle of the night and felt it kick me. That was good — just me and the baby in the dark.'

Clearly there is a dissonance between the men's failure to go to parentcraft meetings (only 9 per cent had done so), which as we met it in the last chapter was often practical and not generally unreasonable, and this urgent drive to be, in ways new to our time, part of the creation and arrive at a within-the-womb knowledge of their child. Nonetheless there were the fathers who said no. The couvade experience might be sharp and surprising to Robin Carter, but to Michael Hahn it was not there. 'Naw. No problems. Hit the hay, flat out. But *her* — she wakes up a lot, she tells me. Natural, she's pregnant and I'm knackered.'

So, despite this mosaic of feelings, ninety-one did not attend parenthood classes. Now, thirty-three announced that they would probably not attend the birth. Sometimes this was news to the woman. The question had never been asked or answered. 'Dunno,' said Gary. 'I mean, no. I'm not going. Nothing for a bloke to do. Maybe when the kid's older. . . . No, I'll ring for the ambulance.' Cheryl joined in: 'Well you take it as it comes, don't you. You don't *need* all these things. It's up to *him* to decide whether to be there. I expect when it comes to it, I'll be wondering. But I expect he'll let me know.'

Other couples too shared thoughts about the birth, but didn't quite connect. 'Don't know if I'll go. Depends on work. Depends on what I'm doing. I'm not keen on blood, either.' To which she coolly replied: 'He doesn't know, so I've asked my dad. Is that all right? Will he be allowed in the labour ward? He was really chuffed when I asked him, but some of my friends, well, they acted like it was peculiar. Is it?'

The answer is no. Women often mentioned to me the idea of someone else close to her being present. A mother came first, but they also turned over the thought of their father, a friend, a family gathering — children and all — or even a pet. Only most rarely were these imaginings translated into actions, but nevertheless they were a first pointer to changing sensibilities. The arrival of the father at the birth bed is so recent a phenomenon that it is understandable that many men live happily within the old separated roles. Yet it is equally understandable that we are now meeting not so much the 'new father' as some less certain, exploring creature which has come with our time and our culture. More than once one might be reminded of those lines of Robert Graves on the progress of butterflies:

> *He lurches here and here by guess*
> *And God and hope and hopelessness.*
> *Even the aerobatic swift*
> *Has not his flying-crooked gift.*

Nevertheless, in this essay on fresh forms of masculinity and of fatherhood, it would be an error (especially after the numerical data in Chapter Two) to underestimate the force of tradition, of inertia and of the micro-complexities of life. Sam Harding walked me down the garden path from his rural bungalow. He had been very helpful to his wife, concerned at attaining a higher level of material life, worried about money and work. He had every value and perception of the traditional father, and the pressures on him were too strong and short-term and crisis-laden for him to sniff any winds of change. 'Come back soon,' he said; 'always enjoy your questions. Takes my mind off matters. I'll tell you now — couldn't back there — but I need a baby . . . like a fish needs a bicycle.'

PART THREE

Coming Up for Air

8
Nativity

'The miracle of reproducing the human species is principally a female miracle. The hormone patterns in a woman's biology reflect this and it is like refusing to look through Galileo's telescope to deny the evidence that is there before us.' I read this in *The Times* of London on the misty November morning when three of these fathers were later that day to feel a different emphasis in the birth of new life.

There had been false alarms. Robin had rung up the doctor 'because Sally had been complaining of stomach pains. He just advised rest and aspirin. The next day when I came home from work, she was much worse, so I rang him up again and said "Look here, she's really distressed." "OK," he said, "bring her in." When he had a look at her he diagnosed appendicitis, and got her in the hospital right away. God, that was panic stations. Imagine having your appendix out *and* a baby at the same time. They were talking about Caesarians and things like that. God, I wouldn't like to go through that again. But after two days it all went away. The cervix had dilated a little, but they said, "Maybe there'd been a touch of gastro-enteritis." The only good thing that came out of it was when they wired her up to the monitor and I saw all that. Not that I could understand the readings. Nobody explained them. The baby books don't have all this mechanical side in them. But come B-day, I won't be so taken aback.'

Meanwhile, Alan felt intuitively that his wife was about to go into labour. He could read her more delicately than the doctor. 'I noticed her mood and the next day mentioned what I thought to the fellas at work. "That's it," they said, "sure sign." I knew before her. That night we were watching TV, and after a while she went upstairs to the lav, stomach pains. She was sure it was stomach pains and nothing else. But I thought, "Aye, aye, here we go." So we went back to the telly, and just after it finished, going up to midnight, she really started.'

All in sequence the fathers suddenly found that pregnancy was coming to a rapid end — and open fatherhood was just over this next range of hills. 'It's really raced by,' mused Robin, not noticing the look that Sally flashed at him.

All these three were warm, tender, concerned men. But yes, by dusk they expected to be spectators at a divine, feminine and professionally staged miracle. First though, there was detailed work to do. No man here had been given the simple factual mechanical information he needed to get the woman to hospital and set himself up to help. Of course they each worked it out, to varying degrees. They needed to know how to call the taxi or ambulance, where to find the bus, or check that their car would start, have petrol in the tank and a place to park. There was a suitcase and a medical file to pick up in the hallway, coins in back pocket for the telephone calls to relatives, telephone numbers in the wallet so that Aunty Mary was not forgotten, maybe food and a flask so that they didn't faint from sheer weariness and heat, maybe a book to read or cards to write, a camera to clutch in the hope you might record the outcome of the miracle.

Urgent, practical, planned detail. The man moves into action. And yet there was something quite wrong about it all. Each father made his own critical arrangements: some surprised, some foreseeing, some superbly, some in a stupor. But why had they not been helped to prepare long ago? A simple leaflet would have eased a lot of worry. After all, they often knew all the particulars of labour stages and breathing patterns. Nevertheless great stretches of their side of the partnership were, like the morning, misty. It was not just a lack of simple advice about preparedness. It was a passing symptom of that unquestioned outlook on the child which — not in any jealous or hostile spirit — simply forgot about father.

Once he reaches the hospital, he meets a well-honed professional procedure. He hands over medical dossier, suitcase and woman, and waits around outside whilst she is prepared (sometimes ritually prepared as with the shaving of pubic hair) elsewhere. 'I was carrying her bags and things, just behind her and I must have gone too far because suddenly they said "You can't come in here" and took them and her off me. *That's* when I felt, well, left out: but you've got to look at it from their point of view.'

For most of them there was to be a lot of waiting about, for which they were poorly prepared, and as their anxiety mounted they often resented little details which give them a sense of being unimportant. 'It was a long, long time. There was no coffee, there was *no* coffee, the machine was on the blink. I wouldn't want to live it again, not like that.' These remarks sometimes seemed like a narrowing concern with their own creature comforts when their wife was in real and not sympathetic labour. 'You need soft chairs. Plastic ones get a bit tough after twenty-two hours, and a room where you can relax, kip when nothing's happening, and decent food, a canteen or some such, not a sandwich machine that isn't working.' But they made these comments so abundantly, and I saw so many variants of this slightly complaining behaviour (rueful remarks about missing a favourite television programme, or mildly complaining about a headache and wondering whether you could get aspirins in a hospital in the middle of the night) that I suspect it would be a mistake to dismiss them like that. These were symptoms of anxiety about the woman. They were also details illustrating how the environment had not been fully shaped so as to bring the man as strongly as possible into the birth.

Most fathers were taken aback at the sheer length of labour. The average time here was 8 hours for the first stage and 30 minutes for the second, though that average conceals much shorter and longer extremes. They had been told, if not at the seldom attended antenatal class then by the woman or by the baby books, to expect as much. What they did not expect was how slowly the seconds ticked by. Sometimes they were sent home. 'It all seemed an eternity, waiting. This young midwife told me to go away and sleep for a few hours. My parents live ten minutes from the hospital, so I went there. At half past five in the morning the midwife rang me, and said it was time for me to be there. I was really still asleep when I answered the phone. It was unreal driving through the empty streets of the city and wondering if I'd be too late. But it wasn't like that. There was a long time to go yet.'

At other times, labour slowed down and the woman was held in a waiting ward. Some men would go away at this point; others like Robin Carter stayed and acted as wholly absorbed intermediaries between woman and staff — often most usefully. 'They put her in a ward, not the labour ward. The contractions were a long way apart and she wasn't all that sure herself. But then it began to change and I could see she was in trouble. She was in pain and they seemed to be coming all the time, and nothing was being done. I could imagine the baby being born there and then, and all the sisters and nurses hurrying around, not even noticing. So I found the sister and said she was distressed. That was the only time anyone was testy. "We're very busy," she said; "we can't be looking after everybody all the time." But it wasn't *everybody*, it was my wife, and anyway I was right. "Please go and look," I said; "she's in no condition to attract your attention." They did, and had her in the labour suite in a trice.'

The procedure next is that the father goes into the delivery room with his wife, unless it is to be a Caesarian — in which case he is excluded. He is dressed in a gown, cap and mask, and stays seated at the top of the delivery room close to the woman's head. He doesn't have a great deal of space. But he is able to offer her sips of water, hold her hand, wipe her brow, rub her back, help to position her on the bed and he may help with giving her entonox (gas and air). The room temperature is high so as to help the baby's body gently adjust from womb heat to hospital heat.

The plan is to clean up the baby, wrap it in a warm blanket and lay it across the mother's abdomen until the delivery of the placenta. The baby is next offered to the father for a few minutes. The midwife then takes the child for weighing, for tagging and for banding of the cord. During this the parents are offered a drink. When the baby is returned, the medical staff retire and leave the threesome alone for about ten minutes. The mother and baby are then wheeled to the post-natal ward, and the father departs to tell the world the news.

The father does not help deliver the child, nor is he encouraged to photograph or record the birth. This is the standard scenario in a British hospital in the early 1980s.

But if that was the backdrop and blueprint for the birth, the individual male experiences could be both intensely different and yet classified in such a way that similar and predictable patterns began to emerge. To begin with the differences, here are some of the men we have met in the previous chapters. Now we join them at the birth itself and listen to how they saw it.

First of all, Adam Smith. It was Adam who had amazed his wife by saying that the time in pregnancy that he liked best was when *she* was asleep, and there was 'just me and the baby, in the dark'. Now he was to meet the child he had so enjoyed in secret anticipation.

'First thing the sister said to me was: "Have you brought any sandwiches?" I hadn't. "Well, it'll be a long night," she said. And she was right.

'I kept finding myself nodding off, even when I was with Judy. Then I'd be back with a jerk. Several times I'd walk like a zombie to the loo. Just taking little steps, stopping at the windows and looking at lights still on all over the city. Just to get away from it for a while, and snatch some fresh air.

'Then when we went in, the sister told me to look after her top half and they'd look after her bottom. So I held her hand and mopped her brow and watched the monitor and gave her water. Then gas. She kept breathing at the wrong time and I could see how they would run out of patience. I kept telling her and telling her, and in the end she got it right. I felt a bit like a doctor.

'And then when it came, I shed a tear or two. Well . . . quite a flood. It was all wrinkled, like a prune — only blue. Didn't expect that. His temperature was high, and wouldn't come down. They took him in the special care unit for two days. They did the right thing. I could visit him all the time, so it didn't make any difference. Best to be sure.'

So the unknown being in the dark was now this smallish, wrinkled, bluish baby in the special care unit. After seven days, he thrived.

Another father on the day was Robin Carter, who had shared the false alarm, but returned grateful for having glimpsed the unexpected high technology of a delivery room, often so far removed from the homely, follow-the-instructions, breathe-in, breathe-out, intimate farmhouse ambience of the baby books. He was waiting to meet 'Adam David — or if it's a girl, it'll be Emily'. But 'It wasn't like that. Sally was finding the breathing and the contractions very hard, *and so was I*. She was whacked. She had this irresistible urge to push, and they'd say "No, not yet." At one time she said "Rob. Let's go home" — right in the middle of labour. But she meant it. So I was getting pretty upset, and then they gave her the epidural. It's magic, that epidural. It just took away all the pain from around her thighs.

'Then it was much easier. I mopped her brow and held her (and watched the machine). That machine worried me. I just didn't know if it was normal for the foetal heartbeat to go up and down as much as that. The only thing that reassured me was that they had two visiting American doctors there. I thought: "Well, they wouldn't be using it as a showpiece if something was wrong. Or would they?"

'Then came the bit I hated. I just didn't want to look. When they cut her. I will always have the memory of that in me. Of course Sally won't. At this moment, in a lot of it, she just wasn't there. I thought "They seem to know what they're doing", but before I could think anything, the baby was *out*.

'But *out*. It was all so rapid. They said something about its head being misshapen, but that would go quickly — and he opened his bowels on the way out — and swallowed the stuff — and the paediatricians were explaining it all — but *not to me* — but to these visiting American doctors.

'The sister said: "It's a girl — no, it's a boy." God knows why she hesitated. The first thing I saw was his testicles. Like a sudden close-up in a film.

'I felt like crying. I really did. But I said to myself: "No, not now. Not with all these people here. Pull yourself together. Not now, not here."

'I felt relief, thankfulness, all rolled into one.'

Another father was Michael Hahn. He was the man who when Clare became pregnant reported: 'I put on a stone — maybe two — rightaway. Too much eating and drinking. But I have no problems. Hit the hay, flat out.' Now he found it all far different from his expectation.

'They knocked Clare out with an injection. I didn't *do* nothing really. Just there, with *her*. It was a long time: perhaps I hadn't really thought of that. I don't think I was in the way, except maybe once. It was like on the film or on TV. I can't say what it was like. It was one of life's experiences. Dunno if it mattered like. I was there, glad I was, though.

'When she came round, *I was holding the baby*. Never expected that. Did it matter?'

Later Clare was astounded to hear all this. So different and so often unshared are the man and woman's perception.

Clare: 'Mattered! It would have been — what's the word — *unthinkable!* Yes, unthinkable for him not to be there. Yes, it did matter. He had to be there. I couldn't have done it without him.'

Mike: 'Mmmmm. . . . Didn't do nothing really. Well . . . I couldn't, could I?'

Clare: 'Yes, you did. You were there, and we did it together. We've always done everything *together*. Even if we just wanted to get a sparking plug for the car, we've gone to get it together. Well, this time it was the baby. Of course it mattered.

Mike: 'Oh. Well. Mmmm. . . . That's what I think too. . . . Mmmm. . .'

Nine months back, Ben Sutherland had been 'a bit surprised when the lump came. I thought well, it's my baby, but no, I don't like it. It's not the woman I married. I'll be glad when she's slim again.'

Now he was to meet 'the lump' and see Lucy find her shape. 'I had to go in with her. I was worried before, expected lots of blood around but it weren't that way at all. I didn't think it'd take so long, though. It was ever so hot and she got real thirsty. They gave her some water, but that was warm, worse than useless. She was doing all the breathing and pushing and things, and she says to me, "Give me that boiled sweet you have in your pocket." I'd forgotten about that sweet. That did her good. Refreshed her.

'But then it came to the gas and air. That fairly chucked me, that. I didn't like to see her going through that. I held her hand and mopped her brow. It were all very slow at first but then, at the end, it was so fast. I didn't really know what was going on. And it wasn't the time to ask, like.

'Then, right sharp, they pulled it out. I thought summat were
wrong. It were all black, bluish. But they said it were OK. No one
told me about the colour before. Nurse said she were OK — but
I counted her fingers a second time to make sure. I didn't cry. I didn't
feel choked. I didn't feel nothing. Queer feeling, good feeling. Can't
explain.'

At the antenatal class, Derek Kennedy had been warned: 'If you faint,
we've no time to attend to you. We'll just step over you and get on
with it.' So he approached the delivery with some apprehension. All
the more so when the doctor decided at a very late stage that it had
to be a Caesarian, and he was left outside.

'I knew nothing about Caesarians, what to expect or anything.
Nurse told me to just wait and if I hadn't heard anything after half
an hour or so, to ring this bell. One good thing about it was you
have a definite time — like a 7 o'clock kick-off — when you knew
it would be born. As it turned out, I met the porter who had wheeled
Maureen in, and *he* told me I'd got a baby girl. I would have liked
to have been told as soon as it was born, not half an hour afterwards.
I suppose they were cleaning it up, they've got their job to do.

'Maureen was still under the anaesthetic and she was a queer colour
— like that shade of grey telephones that you see. I wasn't prepared
for that, and that worried me a lot. She didn't have an epidural,
it was a full anaesthetic. So that meant *I was holding the baby when
she came round*!

'I wasn't prepared for the way the baby looked either. I expected
wrinkles, but it was all puffy, like a boxer, and it had a really red
nose. But most of all I was surprised that its eyes were already open
— and it seemed to be looking at me.'

Almost all the fathers who attended the birth reached an ecstatic
peak of emotion: a personal Everest. Often this was at the moment
of birth itself, sometimes it came an hour or two later as the shock
passed through their system. Then for some while afterwards, their
behaviour was manic, disordered, high. 'I felt like an astronaut who'd
landed on the moon.' Even the more withdrawn ones became
voluble, often drawing total strangers into eager conversation. So
powerful was the feeling that almost every man cried. Some did this
quite openly, some brushed away the tears or sought to conceal them.
The taboo against men's tears is fierce, and for many this was the
first time they had cried since they were small children themselves.
We checked the accuracy of this by observing fathers at twenty
successive births. Eighteen were crying. The other two were numbed:
perhaps their tears came later. 'I had these swellings in my throat,

either side, and I couldn't speak.' There could be no clearer indicator
of their capacity to feel for both mother and child. During labour
their attention, as these quotations show, had moved away from
themselves (where it often was during the waiting period) and on
to the women. So much so that the actual arrival of the child had
an element of surprise — 'It popped out!' Now it focused on the baby,
and several mentioned an odd sensation of suddenly feeling older.
Adam Smith said 'Before, you think a baby is a baby is a baby. But
no. I felt at once: "*He's my son.*" ' Anthony, the thatcher, ruminated:
'I felt — it's hard to say — we've been married for years and I've
always been a fairly hardworking man, but when Jenni was born,
I felt — I know it's silly — but I felt I'd just grown up, there and
then.' They were fathers.

The first action these fathers took after the birth was to scan the
child for any physical handicap. Sometimes you will see a father,
finger outstretched, counting the baby's toes and fingers — one, two,
three, four, five, full set — very much as a small child might. But
this did not entirely reassure them. They were taken aback by the
appearance of their newborn. It was so different from the Christ-
child in Nativity paintings or the thousands of fair, clear-skinned
smiling babies that they had seen in advertisements, on television,
magazines or baby book covers. It was often bluish, wrinkled,
blotchy, marked from the birth. One baby had a tooth, and the father
was suddenly uncertain whether this signalled something seriously
wrong, or whether he had a genius on his lap.

With normal deliveries, the couple were told their baby's weight,
length and Agpar score soon after the birth. The high Agpar score
in particular should have wholly reassured them. One minute after
birth, the child is scored out of ten on the following scale (a different
colour test is used for non-white babies).

	0	1	2
Pulse	Absent	Below 100	More than 100
Breathing	Absent	Slow, irregular	Good cry
Muscle tone	Limp	Some flexion of extremities.	Active motion
Response to stimulation	None	Grimace	Vigorous cry
Colour	Blue, pale	Body pink, extremities blue	Pink all over

But hardly any of the fathers knew what an Agpar score was, so when they were told Agpar 8 or Agpar 9 — in other words a normal healthy child — it was gobbledygook. The weight too was clearly given, but in grams: 'She weighs 3,501', which almost all the fathers (taught to think of babies in terms of seven-pounders or eight-pounders) found incomprehensible. Thus, even at such a keen moment, was the bafflement of father and the mystique of medicine duly preserved.

Almost instantaneous with their darting examination for defect was the sensation of gender. Several fathers mentioned how the boy's testicles, the girl's vagina, as the baby was held up flashed on their vision as if they were seeing them through a zoom lens ('this sudden sight of red testicles'). It was very common for fathers to be 'certain' of the child's sex before it was born. Usually they were 'certain' it was a boy in the womb. Saul Wogan said: 'I knew it was going to be a boy before it came. I just knew it. So when it came I wasn't mistaken, I wasn't surprised. It was the boy I expected,' But, as Derek Kennedy found, you could be wrong. In a taken-aback tone he announced: 'It's a girl — Louise. We both expected a boy. So a girl's a real surprise.' This 'certainty' applies to some mothers too, and can even persist after the birth, as it did with Derek's wife, Maureen. 'I kept thinking it *was* a boy. A few days after it was born, they came round and said there was a service in the hospital chapel, and did any of us want to go. Well, I'd got nothing to do, so I went along. And afterwards the chaplain asked me what I'd had, and I said — straight out — a boy. The mother next to me said, "Oh no, you didn't, it's a girl." And I said, "Oh yes, it is. It's a girl." Really we shouldn't call it "it".' During my visits to this couple, they had called the unborn child 'he', the newborn 'it', and the child they took home 'she' — as expectation and reality fused into one.

This search for the first-time boy seems persistent. The sex of the child can be ascertained before birth, expecially if there is a test for Down's syndrome. I have come across American reports, though how carefully documented they are is hard to say, where it is claimed that, given this knowledge, requests for abortions for a female foetus rise much faster than for a male. That, though, might be more a mother's than a father's decision.

Perhaps there is a second, curious indicator of the father's reaction to the sex of his child, and we return to this in the next chapter. This is the way he holds the baby. Close observation shows that babies and small children are not held haphazardly. Holding positions, to which little conscious thought is given by the parent, may — from the moment of birth — be highly stylized. At least five positions can be distinguished. The most common is to hold the baby in the elbow crook or on the knee. The least common is to hold the baby, perhaps across an arm or knee, so that it is looking downwards. The other positions are holding the baby so that it is looking away, with its back to you; holding the baby over the shoulder; and holding the baby in front of you so that you are looking eye to eye.

Do fathers tend to hold sons and daughters differently? It was impossible to measure this at birth here, but it did seem as if they might. The difference seemed to be that the mother held the baby more closely than the father anyway. But that the father tended to hold a girl child protectively close, whilst a boy child was held more at a distance, as if being inspected, and was more intensely gazed at, eye to eye. They often spoke with wonder at the sensation of first holding and gazing at their child, and the ancient feelings welled up. Just as the women had the sense of an ending — pregnancy was over — so the men felt a beginning: fatherhood was here.

'The baby makes you feel immortal. Well, not quite that. One day the world will blow up and there'll be nothing except atoms and electrons. But down those millions of years your children have children who have children. Yes, you know you will die, but you also feel immortal — you live through that child. That's how I feel about Timothy.'

9
Being There

Being there was a supreme moment. The fathers at the birth took
the baby. They smiled almost all the time. They stroked, inspecting
everything from fingernails to testicles — 'Amazing — it's all there,
in working order'. They were astounded at the softness of the skin
and the blueness of the eyes. Spontaneously they began that first
conversation: 'Tall girl . . . quiet, ain't you? Tall, cuddly . . . cuddly
. . . cuddly . . . cute, cuddly baby . . . pretty eyes . . . choo choo
. . . sweet, ain't you?'
    At first they spoke as if to an adult, but this then changed to this
intimate whispering; and next to a higher-pitched baby talk. This
shift of pitch was universal and fascinating. It seemed to fit in with
the baby's sensitive auditory range, and its attraction to higher
frequencies. I very much doubt if any of these fathers were aware
of this. Nevertheless they were adjusting within minutes or so and
offering the child all the stimuli of touch, attempted eye-contact, and
even sucking ('I wet my finger — like this — and put it in his mouth'),
as well as the right voice. They did not look like the _tabula rasa_ they
are commonly presented as being in the baby books. To some extent,
they seemed to have the elements of fatherhood in their blood. It
was a lovely welcome into the world.
    And yet they came in very different types. In Chapter 2 we saw
that by the time the child was five fathers clearly clustered into the
absent, the traditional, the helping, the tender. So it was at birth.
The first were the refusers. They refused to attend the birth or came
reluctantly; they pushed away all interest in baby lore or the
generative working of the woman's body. Their attitudes to sex roles,
to authority, to discipline were all alike — traditional. Usually they
had distanced themselves from the birth and the future child, as early
as conception. If their attitudes were ever to be changed

it was unlikely that even the impact of birth would do it. Any change needed to come earlier. For after conception they were embarked on what has been called 'the strategy of disavowal'.

We have heard their voices all along, like a running pattern in this tapestry of experience. Ed Kolinski, who told me: 'It was an Insemination Event.' Or Gary, who said, 'Nothing for a bloke to do. Not till the kid's older. No, I won't go. Take it as it comes, like.' Nelson Owen had remarked, 'No, I don't know if I'll be there when it's born. I don't think so, but I hadn't thought about it. There's not much I could do anyway.' Or the wife who looked at her husband and said, 'It's up to him to decide whether to be there, I expect when it comes to it, I'll be wondering if he'll be there. But I expect he'll let me know.' He did. And he wasn't.

Some of these refusers did turn up, but with some distaste or hostility. Whilst one wife was in labour, she squeezed her husband's hand. He drew it back sharply, took off the ring and sucked and licked his finger continually through the rest of labour. He cried when the baby was born, but the ring was conspicuously put on one side, and a private fuss made of putting it back. One did not have to be a great psychologist to read the symbolism of that scene. Nor to notice the rough language in which Ian described his reluctant presence. 'I just dumped her and went off for a kip. When I came back, they kept me an hour waiting. But I thought, like Captain Mark Phillips said on the TV, I felt it was degrading for a woman. All that mess coming out. Count me out next time. Leave it to the professionals.'

The second type of father was the observer. 'We've both seen babies on TV, so it'll be all right, I should think. Let's see,' said one beforehand. At the birth he maintained the same attitude. 'There were no surprises. I've seen it all on the box, so it was as per normal. They were very polite when they were using the forceps. Blood got somehow splashed on her forehead. The doctor wiped it away himself and said "sorry".'

This attitude of being merely an invited spectator was incomprehensible to the last two types of father. Robin Carter had seen it on the film shown at the antenatal class. 'I wouldn't like to be like that father we saw on the film. When it was born, he just said to his wife: "Congratulations, you've had a boy." Just as if it was nothing to do with him. Like something she'd grown in the garden.'

The third type was the sharer. He wanted to know everything. Like Bob Young, who in an earlier chapter told me: 'No, I've never been to the hospital or these classes. I wait till Liz comes back, and then I want all the news. Really drain you dry, don't I Liz?' They were often tinkering with the car to make sure it was ready for the hospital run; they picked up the baby books and asked questions; they took a keen interest in the babies of friends, and shared the breathing exercises with their wife. Often they were like sports coaches, telling her to move her breathing to 'level C' and timing her with a stopwatch. At the hospital they regretted not having been shown how to read the monitor, and were delighted when they were allowed to play an active part. 'I really liked it when they let me help a bit with things — the tubes, the trace and so on.' They were an immense support to mother all through their often unanxious, logical and above all *doing* approach. They were determined to be equal parents from the beginning.

The fourth type was the father who totally identified with the woman. Almost certainly he was stunned and fascinated by the pregnancy. Very probably he went through a sympathetic couvade — and recognized it. In labour he was anxious that the medical staff gave her the best and immediate treatment, and would speak out for her if he didn't think that was happening. He was upset at her distress, and lived the labour with her. Robin Carter, who was in this category, put it like this: 'In the labour suite I caught myself several times, clenching my fists, going red in the face, bearing down, I had to consciously stop myself. Fortunately nobody noticed — they were too busy — or I'd have felt a fool. But I couldn't help it.'

With these four types of fathers we begin with a flurry of actual examples. But the more the evidence is refined, the more one can see them as abstract types, and begin to forecast future behaviour with the child. The reluctant type pushes the whole pregnancy and birth to one side, and finds security in traditional roles: man the hunter, woman the nurturing home. He speaks of a strong distaste, which he may not be able to overcome, of the whole physical process. Mentions of pain, blood, aversion and even disgust come into his vision, even if these are far removed from what actually happens with the mother. Nevertheless this man is the one who most asserts the machismo image. He may be interested in inter-male violence, perhaps in sport. Yet, tattooed, hairy-chested, assertive amongst men, he strongly draws back from this stretch of fatherhood. ('My old man's a butcher,' puzzled one wife, 'but he won't have anything to do with this. Said it would turn his stomach.') The observer type so often mentions having seen the experience before — between the pages of a book, on television, in a film. He may be nonchalant, passing it off as something to be expected and not all that out of the ordinary. He has the capacity to distance the experience just far enough for it to reach a neutral point. He can move closer or further away from it all: not retreating, like the first type, certainly caring at several levels — but not letting himself become wholly involved. He too tends to have a fairly clear idea of divided sex roles. Not so much in a macho sense, but more a belief in them as an efficient partnership in life.

The third type was the sharer. He was very much in evidence in Chapter 2 where he was picking up children from school, sharing the shopping, looking after them when the mother was at work, reading them bedtime stories. All that lies ahead of him. But here he is caught up in the business of birth, and would like to be more involved if only the demands of work, his own lack of knowledge, and the different resistances of women and the medical profession allowed him to grow in that way. He is the man who has seized the new opportunities to attend a hospital birth. The last type, who wholly identifies with the mother, would probably prefer a home delivery to a hospital one. But the professional pressure against it is very strong and he is persuaded by arguments about the safety of such a birth. Nonetheless, in the past, he would probably have welcomed the departure of midwife and doctor from his home, and the chance to be left alone with child and mother. He appreciates the high technology of modern hospital birth, but, faced with machines, drugs, bureaucracy and standardized medical procedures, is not so sure that this yields the quality of experience for which he seeks.

If those are basic types, the next question is: What is their proportion, one to the other? And which are growing, which declining? It is hard to be certain about the latter because we know so very little about the male experience, even in the recent past. But with these 100 fathers, it would be reasonable to say that around 20 per cent were the reluctant type and another 20 per cent were observers. If we put both together, we had the 'traditional' father. Of the remainder, the biggest group of all — 50 per cent — were the sharers, and the smallest — 10 per cent — were the ones who totally identified. If we put both these together, we have a profile of the emergent 'modern' father. This gives the balance in favour of the modern father.

Is this then a trend? All the indications were that it was, and is. Indeed, the changes over even one generation seemed surprisingly substantial, and later we can summarize the major, determining reasons for that. The reluctant ones gave all the appearance of a hard core. I could not see that relatively simple approaches such as informative literature, male-oriented antenatal classes, a wholly welcoming atmosphere at the maternity hospital, or even the continuous pressure of their wives were likely to erode their attitudes. Their position was entrenched and would only shift across generations. If one took the view that the values of the modern father were to be preferred, then this hard-core sense is a measure of achieved change and progress. For in complete contrast, the observers seemed to be in a soft position. They were defensive rather than aggressive. They sat on fences, and were clearly open to persuasive pressure from the general climate of opinion, from the woman and the professionals, and from their own curiosity. Many who said they would probably not attend the birth, but finally did so, came from this grouping.

It looked as if the big shift is from the observers to the sharers, now the pre-eminent group. As for those who identified so wholly, their numbers were perhaps slowly increasing. But they were beginning to ask other, more radical questions about birth and childhood, the relation between the sexes, and between the client group and the professional phalanx. They would, and may, lead us quite elsewhere.

This chapter has taken us inside the hospital; and it is remarkable how the hospital has colonized birth in our time, much as schools colonized education in the nineteenth century. The first recognizable maternity units in Britain were established a hundred years before in the eighteenth century, and by the 1920s over 80 per cent of children were still being born at home. But throughout the industrialized world the post-war years first of all showed a huge shift from home to hospital. By the 1970s, 96 per cent of babies were born there and the figure for first babies was 99 per cent. Only 1 per cent of Japanese babies arrive at home, 2 per cent of West German ones, 3 per cent of Canadian ones. Even in Holland, which has the strongest tradition of home birth, half the children now arrive in hospital and this proportion is rising by 2 per cent each year.

The second big change has been the presence of the father at the birth. As recently as 1970 the majority of hospitals in Britain and the United States refused to let the father attend. The first cracks in the system often came when doctors themselves were allowed special dispensation to witness their own child's birth. But the pressure became irresistible and our hundred fathers here are a fairly typical modern group. When I first met them, two-thirds — 67 — already openly intended to be there. In the event, four-fifths — 82 — were present. From zero to over 80 per cent, within a decade, is evidence, repeated elsewhere, of a shift in the expression of male feeling and male commitment.

The doors of the labour suite are opened. One mother here wanted her own father to be present. Others wondered about relatives, and during the course of the research another maternity hospital had to invent a collective noun to include lovers, lesbian co-habitees, sperm donors, friends — and even husbands. They were all classified as

'labour partners'. Another hospital struggled with the question of a
blind mother wanting her guide dog at the birth, and it was quite
common, with experienced mothers on the wards, to hear the pros and
cons of inviting older children along to greet the arrival of their new
sister or brother. But all these realms of possibility are but little
compared with the arrival of the modern father at the birth of his child.

Yet had everyone appreciated what had now happened? I doubted
it. From being excluded, the man was now suddenly accepted. He
was conscious of his innocence, his ignorance, his fears. There he
was, ill prepared, if willing and positive in spirit, thrust into the white
emotional heat of the modern birth. At the same time, there was
no coherent policy for him. Though he felt central , he was treated
as if he were a marginal man. As one American muttered, 'Guys
get pushed to the side like a third-string quarterback.' That is here
in all the detail of these accounts. Men prepare for fatherhood in
a bewildered way. They are then thrust into a modern, high-
technology and partnership birth. It is a violent experience.
Simultaneously their marginality and their machismo are stressed.
Birth over, as we see in the next chapter, the traditional economic
patterns re-form around them, and pull away from this brief
experience of father as very close to father as absentee provider: 'Bye
baby bunting, Daddy's gone a-hunting.'

What is lost in this is not the reality but the full potentiality of
the bond between father and child. That is only one element in the
complex network of family and caring relationships, but at this point
it is, in some senses, a new expressed force. Of course, the love of
father for child has always been there. What we may be seeing and
assessing here is something different: a force as lovely, and apparently
spontaneous, and as wasted as a waterfall, a Niagara or Victoria
whose sudden, passing energy need not so easily disappear.

It is difficult, searching the literature on how children grow, to
find the often vacant place of the father. As we saw in Chapter 1
he can be the invisible man; or, if not an absent ('Daddy's gone to
a sales conference'), threatening ('Just wait till your dad comes home')
or unpredictable being. But the the plain fact may be that none of
the great mother-centred theories any longer wholly fit the evidence.

The child seems not to attach itself exclusively to the mother, but
to have the survival capacity to attach itself to whatever care-offering
people are close. Naturally that still usually means mother. On this
observation, it can also mean father. It could mean others —
adoptive parents, grandparents, and many more. Where we may
have gone astray is in thinking in such exclusive terms: firstly, that
the child related solely to its mother; secondly, that it related to one
primary person.

This is not what we see with these fathers. We meet often with a male potentiality to bond with the child; a male capacity to develop that; the possibility of doubling the loving and motivational force behind the child — and the bizarre situation, perhaps new and peculiar to our own age, in which such forces, as we have seen, can be suddenly unleashed, though often frustrated.

At nativity the man's capacity to give and to commit was revealed in all its unprotected nakedness. Tom Arnold was a rough-hewn docker. When I first met him he would rock on tiptoe, legs splayed, hands on hips. Every conversation with him looked as if it might lead to the last shoot-out in the OK Corral. He had twins: 'I don't bloody cry at silly films and all that. But this last week I've kept doing it. Made a bloody fool of myself at Interflora. Went for flowers and this young girl — only a kid — said, "What colour ribbon do you want, red or blue?" And I said, "Red *and* blue. It's twins." And the tears came again. I felt a fool, but I couldn't stop it. She was only a kid, this girl — eighteen or nineteen — and didn't understand. She looked at me amazed.'

10
Coming Home

'I came home near to tears, dug out the bottle of champagne I'd hoarded for just this day and cracked it with the neighbours. Even as I was clinking glasses of bubbly I kept dashing to the phone and made manic calls to everybody. I couldn't find *enough* people to phone. And then I just collapsed.'

Others moved into more meditative mood. 'I came home, closed the door and sank into the sofa. I kept thinking again and again "You could have had a ten-year-old son by now" and wondering what a blind fool I had been all those years since we first got married.'

As the wild, hyperactive behaviour dissolved into exhaustion, the empty house closed around them. The postman brought congratulatory cards, quick meals were snatched in the kitchen, neighbours and relatives turned up with offers of help — supermarket shopping, pre-cooked stews. Sometimes a mother or sister-in-law moved in and took over the domestic rhythm, replacing the absent wife. But this was infrequent — they waited for the homecoming not of the father but of the new baby, and the men usually resented what they felt as well-meant intrusion. Partly they wanted time to themselves: it was not a moment to adjust to the intimacy of living closely with someone else; and partly they disliked being pushed towards the periphery again. Several protested that they were far better cooks than the cuckoo-in-the-nest relative; or that they knew exactly where everything was to be found; or that by themselves they ran the house 'all shipshape and Bristol fashion'.

Life's punctuation marks were those visits to the hospital. Most fathers — even those who had never imagined home birth — were anxious to be rid of wards and sisters, doctors in white coats and consultants in suits or sober dresses. The ones who had been such active doers before and at the birth were often clearly frustrated, for now there was very little at all for them to do. Ones who had identified so strongly with the birth were sometimes now fussily critical of the hospital, and pressing for a rapid discharge. But reluctant ones still staked out lonely masculine territory, and said: 'She's better off there, lots of good grub and rest — like a hotel holiday at the expense of the state.' Or 'There'd be nothing on for her at home. Up there, she's got other women with babies to natter with, and all them doctors in case there's any bother.'

It was extremely difficult for the men to keep at or near the centre of the stage, and to establish or reinforce that imprint on the infant, the possibility of which had been so dramatically clear to many of them — 'I'm sure she was looking at me and I by golly was jolly well looking at her.' They were seen not as what they felt in the gut, 'fathers', but seen by everyone else involved as 'visitors'. Again one noted the paradox that the modern father was being taken or invited into a vivid birth experience whose potentialities for early nurturing and education we have hardly begun to explore — and then resolutely pushed or pulled away. Very many of the men saw this with sharp clarity. Few of the mothers and the professionals perceived it as other than natural, necessary and inevitable.

So, curiously, in the tired hither-and-thither of these often bewildered days, men found themselves taking stock of new status. Future responsibilities only half-glimpsed in pregnancy were now upon them. The most plain and primitive response was to stare into the bathroom mirror, and speak aloud: 'I'm a father.' Next came the thought (and it enveloped much early feeling) — 'And I'm the father of a daughter', or 'I've a son.' This difference is so powerful and can be so complex that it is worth pausing with these men as the significance sinks in. We have touched on this in pregnancy, and then there was the odd business of how the father held the child at birth, depending on its sex.

In the early months I had asked them directly whether they wanted a girl or a boy. Normally this received a vague and catch-all reply — 'Don't mind . . . welcome both . . . see what the good Lord sends.' But if I came in at an angle, and inquired whether they had yet settled on possible names, a different pattern emerges. 'A name is a kind of face,' said Thomas Fuller in the seventeenth century, and it is true that different expectations cluster around different names. We expect an unknown Gladys to be different from an unknown Sophie, a Darryl not the same as an Andrew. Parents in choosing a name are forcasting their image of their child. Are they also making an oblique statement of preference? Some were brisk and straightforward: 'Tobias for a boy, Clare for a girl' But most others had difficulties. Jack Diamond said: 'If it's a little boy, it's got to be Jack, my name.

It has to be something simple doesn't it, like James or Joseph or Jack. We haven't got around to a girl's name yet.' And they never did. They did have a boy and made him Jack minor, though, as Jack senior said after the birth, 'I don't know what we'd have called him if he was a she.' Whilst not so certain on one side or so blank on the other, Bob Young was puzzled. 'No difficulty about a boy's name. Howard. That's my father's name. We both agreed at once. We're not so sure about a girl's name. But you see, you have more choices with a girl's name, don't you?' Derek Kennedy was not dissimilar: 'If it's a boy, then maybe Alan or Adrian, with Sean — that's my middle name — back in the middle again. If it's a girl, well, we're not clear yet.' Nor was Saul Wogan. 'The boy's name was easy — Adam — with my name in the middle. But a girl . . . we've looked through the baby book, searching. There's *hundreds* of names for a girl.' He got his boy.

Michael Hahn left it rather late. Both he and his wife Clare agreed from the start that it would be a boy, and called it 'Fred' in the womb. When born it would be christened Myles and grow up to be a doctor. But the genetic dice tumbled against the call, and it was a girl. She was called Gail. It was the midwife at the birth who suggested the name. 'I wouldn't have minded a girl *later*,' murmured the father.

Ben Sutherland offered another variant: 'If it's a boy then Lucy and me agree — it's Shaun. But with a girl we'd like Joanna or Michelle or Billy or Kelly or Shauna. Something that's a girl's name, but boyish.' Certainly there were also fathers and mothers who wanted a first-time girl, and others where it hadn't quite come to the surface, as if they were choosing in a baby supermarket.

Robin Carter: 'As soon as she told me, I wanted a boy, but . . . '
Sally Carter: 'I want a daughter!'
Robin Carter (amazed): 'Do you? A daughter? You never said. Well . . . I'm not against it. . . . Don't misunderstand. . . . That takes the biscuit . . . well.'

In any one year in any of the English speaking countries, 80 per cent of all first names will come from a total list of less than 250. Of those, around 100 will be the pool from which the boys' names are drawn, and up to 150 the usual girls' names. Less than 2 per cent of parents give their child a unique name. On the parish register of a church hard by I found scores of christenings of Stephen, Paul, David, Andrew, Matthew, Christopher, Emma, Sarah, Rachel, Claire, Joanne. But I had to look back to the seventeenth century before I found one Quivinia and one Chatonwyne. Certainly no father there risked even a Hyacinth or an Aaron. Names are a clear social indicator, and — with first-born children — especially conservative. Boys' names more so than girls', since there the cycle of fashion moves distinctly more quickly. They have their resilient class differences too: the annual top list in *The Times* is quite at variance with naming popularities in working-class communities, where Wayne may pip Charles at the post.

With these fathers the drift was to print their own name and sometimes a family name onto the son — together with the name which was his own special identity. So the chain of male names linked across generations. The women approved. A daughter too sometimes carried a grandmother's name. There was no example here of a mother handing on her own name to a daughter: the naming link was much lighter, skipping a generation. Clearly an image and expectation of a son was already forming with most fathers and most mothers. But so too was an image of a daughter. When they chose there, they had a sense of abundant, delightful names — a world of seasons (April), flowers (Jasmine), fine qualities (Verity), fairytale (Gretchen), romance (Juliet) and faraway places (Tania). As we have seen, the usual 'pool' is only half as big again as the male one, but it has less restriction — you can trawl all over it, and it changes attractively. This is worth drawing out because, like the birth-hold, it helps us to see in what different ways father views son and daughter.

Both fathers and mothers were discriminating between a boy and girl before birth, and immediately afterwards. But it was the father who was making the stronger distinction. I found it impossible to be numerically precise here about fathers' feelings. It was clear that both mothers and fathers tended to want a boy child first. Fathers desired this more intensely than mothers. Logically about half of them were heading for a degree of disappointment. Yet there was no sense of rejecting a first-time daughter. They still cried in welcome. But there was often extra pleasure expressed at a first son. A boy was a bonus. Researchers with mothers have attempted to put a figure to this phenomenon. Ann Oakley in an excellent study, *Women Confined*, reported that on a completed sample of fifty-five first-time mothers '54 per cent of the mothers-to-be wanted boys and 22 per cent wanted girls (25 per cent said they didn't mind). Of those who had boys, 93 per cent were pleased, compared with 56 per cent of those who had girls.' Perhaps this magnifies small numbers, and it may be a harsher sense of the initial reaction than I record, but nevertheless it is a characteristic example which points the same way.

There is a certain amount of scattered, psychological research which comes close to the unasked questions. None of it establishes or can wholly establish the father's attitude to son or daughter. But, clustered together, many small studies are sketching the same message. For instance, in the United States, Jeffrey Rubin and colleagues took fifteen couples who had just had a son, and fifteen to whom a daughter had been born. They interviewed them within 24 hours of the birth. Usually they saw the man first, since the woman was recovering from drugs. This was in a Boston, Massachusetts, hospital where fathers were not allowed into the delivery room, were not permitted to handle their child in the first day, but could look at it through a display window in the hospital nursery. There was no significant difference in the weight, length or Agpar scores of the infants. Nevertheless the fathers thought — filling in a test scale — that their sons were larger, stronger, hardier, with bolder features and better co-ordinated. They rated their daughters as softer, finer featured, more awkward and inattentive, weaker and more delicate, and a bit more cuddly. Since the men knew nothing of the babies' internal life, and had only seen them through a glass darkly, this is pure external labelling — coming from *within* the father, not from the child: 'nature's first projective test'.

Similarly there have been a number of small experiments in which men (usually students, that docile and untypical regiment of the researched) have been either given a very young child or shown a videotape of one. Some of the men are told it is a girl, some are told it is a boy. They are invited to play with the real child, or give an impression of the one on film. Naturally these are not fathers with their own child so the evidence is much more tangential and I am uncomfortable about the ethics of this. Nevertheless it carries a similar impetus. Offered the chance to play with a 12-week-old child dressed in yellow and told it was a girl (even if it was a boy), men — more than women — at once reached to offer a doll out of the selection of toys at hand, or described the 'girl' as needing protection rather than a baby adventure programme. The indications are that though women and men both have a strong and instant sense of 'girl' or 'boy', even with a child they have not got to know, it is the man — and in this book the father — who has the keener sense. Having established 'boy or girl?' — as he did at the birth moment — he now radiates towards the child an equally loving but strategically significant barrage of signals.

But as the father snatched his sandwich at home, tidied up the room, screwed himself up to go out and buy welcoming roses, fled into retreat with his mates or to the escape of television, he almost always explored the edges of another thought. Yes, he was a father. Yes, now he now had a child who was a boy or girl ('Oh Lord,' said Roger, 'this will go on till I die'). But also — and sometimes for the first time — he compared himself to the only model he knew: his

own father. For the paradox is this. The yearning and emotional offer
from these modern fathers to their first born can be ecstatic. Even
the observers find that you can seldom sit on the wall all of the time,
without the risk of tumbling off. Yet, almost always, they did *not*
want to be like their own father. Their childhood model of
fatherhood had bred a latent or overt anti-model.

As Paula said in Chapter 1, 'My dad was a photo on the mantelpiece. I knew the photo, but I didn't know him.' The mothers had
these thoughts, as they become part of a new family, but perhaps
as the masculine mantle descended on their shoulders the fathers
searched for that remembrance with special eagerness. But memory
could be such a play with shadows. Of the many, troubling and
sometimes unexpected questions which these men met, the most
strange was the simplest. How do you remember your own father in
your own early childhood? It is an exercise which every man can
explore.

Answers dredged from deep memory can be baffling and potent.
Of course the curtains of the mind screen most childhood from us.
But when these fathers travelled back it was usually not only with
difficulty but with surprise.

'My dad? Er . . . that's a good 'un. I know him now, of course.
But when I was a nipper? Well . . . that's a good 'un. I'd like to think
about that. Yes . . . now I think about it, I'd really like to think
about it. I don't really seem to remember my dad — at that time.
He came later. Not when I was a nipper. I remember my mum of
course, but — until you brought the matter up — well . . . he must
have been there.'

Ed Kolinski said: 'My father was invisible to me. I don't want to
be like him. I want to be giving my child confidence.' And similarly
Bob Young: 'I never really knew him as a child. I'd never thought
about it before but I've just calculated that there's the same age gap
between me and the baby as there was between me and my father,
and I want to be closer to my kid, much closer, than he was.'

By 'being closer' they meant imprinting themselves on the child,
being a presence in its early life: 'He stares at my face, fascinated.
He's discovering *me*.' They meant touching, stroking, fondling,
kissing. They meant play together. Robin Carter confessed: 'I'm
daydreaming about Daniel. Maybe we'll play football, float frisbees,
have train sets together. It's kind of licensed when you're a father,
isn't it?'

From being the play companion that they seldom recollected from
their own childhood, they saw themselves prompting and teaching.
'I think of the baby having a talent. Something creative. Something
where I could help a bit. Music perhaps. Noticing things, drawing.
I would take an interest there as soon as I can.'

Again and again they made the same point. Here is Derek
Kennedy: 'I won't be like my own father. Not that I remember him
in those days. Fact is, I'm only just thinking of it. I'd like to teach
the baby. You know, all kinds of things like swimming.'

Frequently they said — looking at or thinking of the baby — that
they did not want to be the authoritarian father of legend. 'I don't
want to come home from work, and hear the wife saying, "Wait
till I tell your dad how naughty you've been today — then you'll
catch it." I want to *be* with my kid.'

How 'close' their own father had been to them in childhood is
impossible to know. Memory selects, stylizes, distorts. Perhaps that
past generation of fathers shared some of this upsurge of emotion;
possibly it was as quickly extinguished. What could Robin's own
father really have felt all those years ago? 'Dad was all right. He
was fine. But he didn't have much to do with us. He was affectionate,
but not close to us. His thing was the Salvation Army, and really
it was mother who brought up all seven of us. Now I come to think
of it, that's funny. Very funny. Because he delivered me.'

11
Baby Days

'I keep creeping in and gazing at the baby. I touch her all over. I touch her even more than anyone else. More than Jacquie, and we're happily married. I want to see her awake. I want to see her looking at me. Sometimes when I touch her, I'm cheating. I'm trying to joggle her up, make her wake — you must admit she's a smashing baby — and I just yearn for her to be awake, all there, alert-like, and we look into each other's eyes. It's all we've got yet, but she stares at me, I dunno what she sees. But I know what I see. My girl.'

So the baby was welcomed home to the nest and most of these new fathers began by yearning to be close to it and to the mother. The overwhelming majority foresaw sunny, tranquil, halcyon days ahead. All the power, wonder and passion that had passed through them could now be transmuted into nurturing and fatherhood. As in the Auden poem when Prospero sails back to Milan:

> *Their eyes are big and blue with love: its lighting*
> *Makes even us look new: yes, today it all looks so easy.*

But easy it was not to prove. First of all came the shadow of work. How much time should or could be taken off work (if you had work) for the birth of a first child? Here are their plans in those early months after conception, and then what actually happened.

We can think of these figures as four blocks. There were those, not at all insignificant, who carried on working. This would include some shiftworkers, and some self-employed men who felt they could reconcile the balance of hours at work and at home. But it also took in some men who retreated from or rigidly refused to adapt to the new event. A second block (who appeared in Chapter 2) were the jobless. They were at home, but unwillingly so, and sometimes facing

A father's time off work for the birth of a first child

	What they planned beforehand	What they actually did
No time at all	9	11
Two days	12	14
One week	26	31
Ten days	3	6
Two weeks	21	21
Up to three weeks	4	4
One month	1	1
Unemployed	7	12
Undecided	17	0

an identity crisis of their own. That leaves us with two further blocks: one very large and one very small. Seventy-two of the fathers took between two days' and two weeks' leave. They are the overwhelming norm. Only five fathers either could take or chose to take more than this.

The experience of the men who did spend that much time at home was not altogether encouraging. The unemployed fathers had great difficulties. Not fundamentally because of financial problems, though those were always there. It was more that the lack of paid work had robbed their lives of the meaning on which it was founded. At the same time too, the wife transformed into mother was replete with an often overwhelming sense of the importance and centrality of her existence. The employed men who stayed at home for a longer time had special difficulties too. They wanted to express the gentler and what we perhaps mistakenly call the feminine side of their nature. They cooked meals, filled the house with flowers, planned little surprises, prepared the bottle, fed the baby and cooed over it in the bath. But they met resistance.

That often came from sisters or mothers-in-law or women neighbours who, for a while moved in or looked in, and without hesitation assumed the regal role, and relegated the baffled father to being 'a good help'. 'He's very domesticated, aren't you, Peter?' was perhaps the common phrase that most made their blood boil. But professional women workers in the field of early childhood were often very similar. Note this vignette between Derek Kennedy and the midwife. Note too his acute sensitivity, reading unspoken words into her looks.

'She comes round. She's a bit sharp — gives orders not explanations. The other day Maureen was in the bath and I was — well — playing with the baby. I went to the door with the baby on my shoulder and her first words were: "What are *you* doing with the baby? Where's your wife?" That sort of thing. I saw her look. As if I shouldn't be there.'

Nevertheless, men freely talked about their new sense of 'being a family' or 'of all us together'. Whether they were still at home or back at work, they were usually intensely curious about the baby. 'I can tell his different cries better than her really. You see it's a kind of code, he's really talking — telling us he's hungry or he wants picking up or he's got wind or he's too hot. I'd never thought of any of that before. I thought they just lay there and yelled. But they don't.' They were fascinated by the eventual colour of the baby's eyes. Ian had a bald little girl with green eyes. 'I can't believe it. When I'm at work I sometimes have these drifting thoughts about what she'll look like as a woman. Magnificent. Green eyes!' They watched the hair fall and grow and change colour as closely as did the mother. They stroked the skin and often when I called made a point of picking up the baby and holding it themselves — even when it might have been better off sleeping. It was an emblem of fatherhood.

Some would rush home from work in time to cuddle the baby in that sliver of time before it disappeared into the broken night. Steve Campbell, who barely saw his child from Monday to Friday and had hardly adjusted his life at all ('I've tried to cut down on my evenings out, but you've got to keep up with ordinary living, haven't you?'), nevertheless relished the prospect of weekends. 'I get the car out, and the wife sits in the back with the kiddy, that's for safety, and we go on these great spins round all the places where we grew up. Fantastic view, and I just know, I know the kiddy's taking it in. Flakes out in the end of course. I love those spins, all three of us in the car. Great feeling.'

And of course there was the wait for the first smile. The conventional wisdom is that a baby begins to smile at about six weeks. That means the smile of recognition, of request, of imitation, of wanting friendliness in a dependent position. All before may be wind and grimaces and trying out the face muscles. But this is not what many of these fathers felt. They spoke radiantly of smiling from their child at three weeks or much earlier: 'You *know* it's a genuine smile when the eyes and mouth match up.' The mothers were noticeably less sure. Perhaps they had read more baby books, or knew more about the contortions in bringing up wind. I am inclined to think the men, maybe reporting with the penetration of the innocent eye, were probably right. 'He stares at my face, fascinated.' I heard variants of that phrase dozens of times, together with many acute, close observations. After little more than two weeks Robin was saying of his son: 'Those eyes are watching me. They watch

other things too, like the light. But they're watching me, all right.
Tell you something else, he's trying to move his neck. He can't really,
it's all loose, but he's trying to pull it round and look. Watch! He
might smile in a minute. I can sometimes get him to do it.'

What is important about this stretch of the male experience is that
it suggests that the sometimes fierce, passionate bond that the man
felt for the child at birth (or the more mysterious one during the
couvade) is developing during these early weeks — if only they have
contact. The child too is responding and the 'bond' being forged,
as it is with the mother, and perhaps could be with other present
and caring people too. With this intimacy between father and child,
there is another strand which is peculiar to our own time, and one
facet of the new father. That is feeding the child.

Almost all of the mothers intended to breast-feed, at least in the
first months. They were sometimes anxious about whether they
would have the milk, or whether their nipples were too retracted
or would work at all. And many a couple later mentioned their
surprise at the nipples spraying like a watering can with a rose filter.
The advice from midwives was usually in favour of breast-feeding,
sometimes somewhat insistently so — physically coupling unwilling
lips to unready nipple. Few of the midwives or young nurses here
had suckled a child themselves.

That advice of course is based on the natural rhythm, and excellent
biochemical evidence that mother's milk, if it flows, is not only
satisfying, cheap and convenient, but a protection against some of
the early ills of babyhood. But it didn't always flow, or, if it did,
painfully. I noticed mothers feeling twinges of guilt. But after the
initial, almost erotic pleasure of suckling the child, they frequently
began to make other arrangements. Sometimes they supplemented
with a bottle, sometimes they abandoned the breast. A few lasted
the course; they were conspicuously either well endowed or highly
educated or extremely determined. One of their husbands said: 'Sue
went out for an hour, and the baby got hungry. There was nothing
I could do except give it my finger to suck. I felt useless, utterly
useless. I was a nothing.' It is not the purpose of this chapter to
balance the pros and cons of the breast or the bottle. Both are often
passionately advanced. The question here is the effect on the father's
sense of woman and childhood. For this is how people actually
behaved.

One sensation was the ambiguity of the woman's breasts. They
all knew perfectly well that they were there, as on other mammals,
to nourish the young. But they knew all that at a school-textbook
or day-on-the-farm level. It was not their sensibility at all. The breasts
were a focal part of the sexual attraction and cultural beauty of the

woman. That was usually true for her as well. So when she melted into feeding motherhood it clearly stirred their inner selves. Traditionally, psychologists point back to their own sunken memories of a mother and being at the breast. But that is not how men articulated their feeling. Piers said: 'You should have seen her. She had a smashing pair. Hope it all comes right again. Good for baby, common sense. Hope she gets her figure back. Like she was.' That distinct sense of loss need not be left to psychology. The men desired a beautiful erotic wife *and* a mother of the child. Judging by the care the women took — the creams, the smoothing away of saggy stretch marks, the exercises — they were seldom in disagreement. What neither wanted, and they said so, was the past life of their parents or grandparents, or the life on the poorer parts of the globe today, where first childbirth was the beginning of the destruction of the woman's body.

That was one aspect of the new experience. But I suspect the next one has more latent consequences. The bottle meant that the father could perfectly satisfactorily feed his own child. They knew this too, and sometimes delivered me learned minilectures on the right temperature and make-up of their child's bottle. Some would get up in the night and take over. Others made treaties. Adam Smith fed their child every night except Friday and Saturday. But the majority in bottle-feeding homes did not share the task. They saw it as a treat, perhaps once a day, perhaps twice, and something in which they usually invested trouble and patience. So far as I could see, it was splendid for the child. And that cameo of so many men hugging the baby to their own sterile nipples and crooning over the full, warm bottle remains in the mind.

One could analyse this in terms of imperfect role-sharing easily enough. Or — as I have heard when presenting this passage at seminars — as a reduction of the woman's identity as mother. But that would be to miss the point. What we are seeing are ordinary men, with all the normal economic and cultural pressures bearing down on them, venturing out and paddling in the shallow margins of the sea. As with a child on his first seaside outing, there is a slightly timorous element of sheer play. It is a novel experience for the common man in the emerging generations; and, when we later come to look at the 'feminine' and 'masculine' side of the father, it is amongst his most important modes of expression towards the young child.

This is the bright side of baby days. The darker obverse is equally telling. 'Tumble into bed, knackered, then bloody hell, it yells at three, no sleepeye till five, then alarm and up for work. I've been a bloody wreck for ages.' Or Michael Hahn: 'The baby really tires you out. She's not really naughty, but when she keeps on crying, there's times when my eyelids really hang down. I'd give anything to close them.' Or Alan: 'He doesn't really, not when you think about it, cry *all* that much. But I can't sleep properly. I don't know if I'm *waiting* for him to cry, or worried in case he's choked himself. I don't mean to, but I can tell you — ask her — I can get really ratty.' Or Bobby, in a weary voice: 'It seems a hundred years since Sophie was born, and yet it's only four weeks.'

It was not hard to see why, on average, one child is killed by its parents every day in the United Kingdom. There was nothing like that here. But, had some of these tensions been so intensified by psychological or economic burdens, it was credible that some of these fathers and some of these mothers could have snapped. Nor was it difficult to see the need for a 'crying baby service' — somewhere you could ring for advice or help if that once-darling baby endlessly screamed in the middle of the night and you had exhausted all your knowledge and spirit. The mother was spent with the rounds of the day, the father with the unexpected domestic demands after a hard day's work elsewhere.

That daily round set many demands. And here the partnership felt the strain so alien from the advertised images of having a first child. There was not only crying and feeding and being anchored to the child by that now invisible umbilical cord. There were those thousands of nappies to be folded, pinned and washed. And bath time. One remembers the nuances in that scene in E. M. Forster's *Where Angels Fear to Tread*. The single-parent Italian father, Gino, bathes his baby son. Miss Abbot, the visitor from England, looks on:

> He walked sternly towards the loggia and drew from it a large earthenware bowl. It was dirty inside; he dusted it with a tablecloth. Then he fetched the hot water, which was in a copper pot. He poured it out. He added cold. He felt in his pocket and brought out a piece of soap. Then he took up the baby, and holding his cigar between his teeth, began to unwrap it. Miss Abbot turned to go.
>
> 'But why are you going? Excuse me if I wash him while we talk. . . . You have not seen him yet.'
>
> 'I have seen as much as I want, thank you.'
>
> The last wrapping slid off. He held out to her in his two hands a little kicking image of bronze.
>
> 'Take him.'
>
> She would not touch the child.

The reality was rarely as dramatic and as romantic as that (if at moments it could be). Nor did many of the men wash the baby or even change nappies at all frequently. Yet, as older parents may know, both can be the most pleasant, intimate and carefree moments of the budding child-and-parent relationship. Not that they did not much more frequently offer. But sometimes they had strong reactions which were not about laziness, and are worth a word. When one man said 'Hell, no. I'll not change a nappy, never. No way, man', I doubt if he was talking about demeaning his masculinity. Masculinity was the hidden subject, but it was more that curious reverse of the male image that we met at birth. The very ones who displayed tattooed strength most deeply felt a fear, a strangeness of the pain, mess and trouble of birth. Most men no longer seem to have this so rooted in them, though once it seems it was the common, cultural response. But some here still did.

More were simply put off by the woman's criticism of their inexperienced effort. If ever there was a simple point to be made to new parents, it was needed here. Only two fathers had ever changed a nappy before their child was born. So much for realistic preparation for parenthood. But then much the same was true of the mothers. Uncertain as they were, they felt compelled to assume the role of experience. They often did this by correcting the father's equally clumsy efforts. He simply gave up, and the sexes retreated to original positions.

And in all this there was always concern about the early ailments of childhood — the threat of a cold or a touch of jaundice, or very tiny matters which, in these strains, were magnified. 'He had these little hiccups. We lay in bed and worried about them. We didn't like to call the doctor or anything. Look silly perhaps. But how could we tell if something was wrong or not? In the end, I just burst out with it at work, and a couple of my mates said, "Hey, it was just like that with ours. Must be normal." So I came home and told the missus what they said, and we were both that relieved. Like a weight lifted off your head. Anyway, the hiccups went, so they were right.'

But for most fathers matters were not working out as they had expected. Sometimes they saw the breakdowns as the new mother not being adequate to the new role. After all the bride-like celebrations of birth, the congratulations and the cards, came this. 'Took two days off when she had the baby, and then went back. But then, when I saw she wasn't coping, I had to take more time off. I couldn't do it at once. It took a while to sort out different problems at work, but it had to be done.'

There were sometimes bouts of tears to greet the man's arrival home, and the vexed question of where to sleep. Should the baby be in a separate room? Should the man and woman sleep separately?

Some, of course, did not have these options open to them, and for
those the tensions could become intense.

It may seem strange to think of new, first-time fatherhood as a
depressing experience. Clearly it has utterly diverse aspects, yet
depression was one of them. It is fairly well documented that mothers
may enter a period of post-natal depression: post-partum blues. Of
men's reactions we know almost nothing. And yet theirs may not
only help us to understand the male, but also to be clearer about
the mother's state. For example, Ann Oakley in her study *Women
Confined* draws our attention to one major medical attitude towards
the birth, not the birth of the baby, but 'the birth of the blues'. She
alerted me to writers such as Katherina Dalton:

> After the birth of the baby the placenta comes away from the
> womb. . . . The additional source of progesterone has therefore
> been removed . . . the woman's body adjusts to a normal
> progesterone level, which is a hundred times lower than the level
> she experienced during late pregnancy. This is responsible for the
> 'puerperal blues' or tearfulness so frequent among women during
> those few days after the baby's birth. The woman . . . may be
> upset by this sudden decrease in her progesterone level and may
> develop a more severe puerperal depression in which she becomes
> apathetic and tearful, losing appetite, interest, energy and
> initiative; she may also become sexually frigid.

Similarly Kaij and Nilsson in their study of 'Emotional and psychotic
illness following childbirth' argue along similar lines. 'To the
observer, the mother appears slightly euphoric, unrealistic,
"whimsical". . . . The slight euphoria, the irritability, the emotional
lability, the stereotyped crying behaviour and the impression of slight
confusion are all, in our opinion, characteristic of the early
postpartum period. We are inclined to interpret these symptoms as
physiological, rather than psychological reactions, perhaps due to
an increased secretion of corticosteroids.'

Almost every couple here had picked up this belief in hormonal
readjustment. Certainly the professionals passed it on as received
knowledge. As I made my visits, there were stories in the media of
the unfairness to women who had to sit examinations at the critical
point in the menstrual cycle, and a woman being acquitted of murder
because that too had occurred at the wrong moment for her
hormonal rhythms. This of course is to blur the menstrual cycle into
the post-partum blues. That is exactly what the couples here believed,
and had been led to believe. Personally I doubt if this biological
argument, at either point, can be dismissed. But it can, and here was,
exaggerated into the universal explanation.

Against this there is a counter-argument that depression in early motherhood (and indeed in later motherhood) is quite as likely to be the result of lack of affection, too many problems, shortage of cash, cramped housing and many other social forces. Twice as many women as men visit a psychiatrist, and depression for mother doubles after birth. A first birth is only one of the dramatic events of life, but it is climactic, and it seems impossible to ignore all these inner and outside strains.

The weakness of this line is that it is, once again, wholly based on the woman's conditions — whether hormones, sexuality or mounting bills. For the striking thing is that the emotional reaction of these fathers was *exactly the same*. They had no periods, nor had they experienced post-partum biological readjustment. They certainly had gone through an upheaval in their lifestyle. And in these baby days two-thirds of them were groggy. Almost all the symptoms recorded for women were their symptoms too. They were gloomy, downhearted, waking up worried in the morning, having to tell themselves 'I should be enjoying this' and recognizing that rather than living an emotional life of constant sunshine theirs more often was an April weather existence: storms and rainbows. If they were different from the mothers, it was in two aspects. They didn't cry, but they were more likely to burst out in anger, or to sulk. One in three of these fathers passed through some clear bout of depression, and none of them could quite understand why. The explanations in ordinary currency simply did not include them. 'All women are like that,' was frequently said. No voice added, 'And all men.'

Fathers did not always give of their best, because, distinctly more than mothers, they were unprepared for the adjustment to parenthood. And they had no one to talk to about it. With their wives they felt it their duty to give support, however cursory, and not lay bare all their worries. There was a curious difference in their communication. The mothers spoke freely to mothers, sisters, friends, neighbours, midwives, health visitors, doctors. They lived in a free-trade area of advice and information. Not so the fathers. Relentlessly they revealed the emotional barrier that lies between men. At the peak of his excitement one father 'talked to one or two other men. My neighbour over there, see? They're expecting and I asked him if he would be at the birth. "No fear mate. Too much bloody blood for me." Amazing what people think. I've never had an experience like that. But if you start mentioning it, someone always shuts you up, or caps it with a horror story.'

More usually, they mentioned that after the first round of formal congratulation and a joke or two 'my mates just didn't want to know. Rather talk about the racing card or our rotten wages.' Ray said:

'I wanted to tell them all about the baby. After all, I hadn't really got anybody to tell, had I? But I soon learned not to. Don't know whether they were bored or embarrassed, maybe just plain not interested.' Here the inhibition is external, but it reminded me of how at the beginning of these early interviews, before the words cascaded out, it had frequently been internal too. Sometimes when I had asked what they felt about the fact that they were going to have a baby, going to be a parent, they had explained with perfect aplomb not what they felt, but what their wives felt. We shall return to this theme in Chapter 13.

But one channel was now and again miraculously unblocked. The drama of birth and parenthood could make their own fathers open up, accept them on new terms, remember their own initiation, and try and gaze into the past and future. I called on Pat Daniel when the grandfather was there, and it was the grandfather who began talking, first about the baby, and then he said:

'He's a wonder. Look at him. Glad he's a boy, aren't you? What'll it be like, his life, do you think? Modern world and all that. Tomorrow's world, I should say.

'I saw five-masted schooners when I was a boy in Bristol. I remember one, after the war, stuck here for a long time with a writ nailed to its mast. I went to sea when I was fourteen. I was so little, my mother carried my box on board. Couldn't manage it myself, couldn't manage it myself. And this big bloke comes roaring round every morning, maybe 4.30, and shouts at me "Ye little bastard, what y'doing still in bed. Get up and get on with it." Talk like *that* to a kid today.

'I don't approve of all that goes on nowadays with children — hooligans and permissive societies — but I hope it's going to be a better world for him. More kind, perhaps.'

Pat turned to me with astonishment as his own father took the baby. 'He's never spoken to me like that all these years. I didn't know any of these things. He used to be mostly silent. And now he's talking to me all the time.'

So fathers found themselves in a world which was at once real and unreal. Very real since it was full of baby and mother, shared or glimpsed joys. Full too of work and weariness, of unpaid bills and endless baths and dirty nappies and fractured nights. The unreality of their preparation for parenthood was breathtaking. In former generations, where men were encased in clear roles, and birth and childhood set apart within the female sphere, this may not have mattered so much. But these fathers were drawn into the novel and modern experience, and not equipped for its traumas. Very unreal too, since, after the clarity of birth, time was often passed in a kind of haze. Something had been lost: old rhythms, former leisure and pleasure, the previous relationship with the woman. All this had seldom been foreseen. The irrevocable nature of parenthood sank in. It is easy to get married; much harder to get unmarried. Still, one can have ex-wives and ex-husbands. But, after that leap from love-making to birth, they discovered that you can hardly have ex-children.

PART FOUR

On the Outside, Looking Inside

12

'The Child Grows Towards the Father'

'From the moment of birth the child grows towards the father,' observed Margaret Mead. Is it so? In the first year it was clear to see what she meant. The mother was a sheet anchor. She fed and changed and comforted the child. Even women who, to their husbands, had seemed distinctly unmaternal responded like this. 'Sue amazes me. She's never been what you might call the lovey-dovey type. I couldn't see her being bothered with the baby. But now she's all over it. Even when she's talking about something else, I can tell, Daniel is always at the back of her mind.' This was true too of mothers who had been very articulate about equality and role-sharing. 'She used to go on about it wasn't going to be _her_ baby. It was going to be _our_ baby and I'd got to agree to pull my weight. Well I did. But I'm lucky to get a look in these days.'

One could argue that to think of the child growing towards the father is to be confined to the past. But that is not what we see here. During these early years it was, in practice, the father who represented the outside world. Yet the concept is not about equal opportunity or the images that our society passes on. It is about the nature of fathering. Perhaps the classical image, snapped in a thousand albums, lodged in memory, is the one of first tumbling steps. Mother releasing the child; father kneeling, coming down nearer child height, arms outstretched, welcoming. It is too ordinary and common a scene to dismiss, and it is not entirely about learning to walk. For what seems to be happening is that the child knows the mother, but is discovering the father. The father too, perhaps with little knowledge of early growth, possibly with little time to share, is both drawing the child towards him and puzzling out their relationship.

Of course that is not how it feels at the time. A first example is play. Father wants to play. Without reflection, most of these men became children themselves for intense if brief spells. They cooed and cuddled, ruffled and rumpled, teased and tossed the child inches in the air. They played imaginary games — giants, elephants, railway engines. In an odd way child and father responded to each other like equals. It was as if a part of men's own childhood had to be relived; or perhaps had never been lived out in the first place. But it was also a rehearsal for the world around. It was usually the father who encouraged slightly risky or more daunting explorations — splashing in water, climbing stairs, pawing the cat, licking strange food. And it was the father who more commonly found the child amusing, hilarious, comical. The mother was more cautious, protective; the man treated the toddler not so much as a child but as a mini-adult. Sometimes you would hear him playfully address it as 'young lady', 'missy', 'young man', 'Master Hamieson'. I never heard a mother refer to her child like that.

There was another verbal difference. It was perfectly common to hear a father speak to the child as 'my son' or 'sonny' or even 'chip off the old block'. Much more rarely, but sometimes, he might say 'daughter of mine' or 'my darling daughter'. Again it was most unusual to overhear a mother talking intimately in such straightforward terms of lineage. This leads to another characteristic of man playing with small child. From the beginning they tend to be not only distinctly more physical, but more aggressive too. I watched Simon playing a ball game with his toddler. The child, swathed in nappies, tumbled over every twenty seconds. All the same, Simon saved and scored 'goals' and both seemed to sense the thread of seriousness beneath the play. There were lots of 'ohs' and 'ahs' and 'well done' and 'try again'. In more than one sense the tiny boy was being taught to stand on his own feet.

This conspicuous interest in 'play' by the father bred a complementary demand from the toddler. When the father appeared the child expected play and, if nothing was happening, made the opening bid himself. Whether this was different between sons and daughters was hard to establish by observation. The fathers appeared more conscious than the mothers of distinctions between son and daughter. They protected the girl, and pushed the boy. Yet this was true of mothers too; and, as men saw something especially fascinating in a daughter, women had a counter-curiosity in a son. There was a criss-cross pattern of identification: a balance. But the makings of cultural gender were there: boys were being gently but insistently made into cultural males; girls into cultural women. In his intense but much briefer relationship with his child, it was the father who most evidently was defining what is expected of a boy, and what of a girl, and how they become unique. At birth the sex had been a sudden surprise. But in these early years it was something which the father built from and shaped and moulded: a pattern not quite the same as he had inherited.

If the man was with the child (and as we saw from the beginning this can be a very considerable 'if' indeed), then one facet of fatherhood, which he defined in action, was play — different from the mother's, full of rougher physical prompts. She might nuzzle, kiss and cuddle more. He tickled, bounced, tumbled — and laughed. The mother often drew in objects to amuse the small child — bricks, rattles, soft toys. A very rare woman just used things about the house.

'Jane doesn't bother about toys much. Not at all. She'll let him play with his bottle. Or give him a wooden spoon from the kitchen rack and one of our new pans, and see what he makes of that. Not that it saves her much trouble. He just can't concentrate that long, and he loses them when they're under his nose, and then the squawking begins again.'

But the father's play with the growing baby was play for play's sake. It drew an immediate response from the child: kitten-like romps of seeking, finding, holding, losing, teasing — and all the time, touch. As we have heard in several of these fathers' voices, there was novelty (far more so than for the mothers) in being licensed to touch a growing child so freely. The emphasis of the mother, by contrast, was, as the child developed, usually more educational, in the special pre-school sense. She would encourage play which meant matching colours ('These are the reds. Find another red. Mmm . . . good girl'), or matching shapes (those endless, frustrating struggles to put irregular shaped objects into odd-looking 'post-boxes'). And, though the mother was bleeping continual signals of encouragement, I was surprised — thinking of man's image of his own authority and as decider on discipline and order — that it was conspicuously the mother who, as the child crawled or toddled around room or garden, kept saying 'No', 'Don't' 'Nasty', 'Don't touch', 'Oh dear', 'Come back', 'Oh no!' She assumed the obligation for preventing danger — better safe than sorry — even when the father sometimes laughed and egged the toddler on.

Yet there were other subtle changes in play as the older children here became toddlers, early childhood was left behind and thoughts of new succeeding babies came creeping into the conversation. The fathers now increasingly drew toys into the play. They had obvious favourites: bricks, balls or almost anything on wheels. We've noticed before the myriad ways in which the father defines and transmits the signals of cultural gender to his child — 'You're my girl', 'This is my boy'. The difference in his degree of aggressive play with son or daughter was one. So too was this reaching for the favoured toy. And with it came something else in which he seized a salient role: the shift from play to game. As the child enters the larger world, play becomes an exciting activity you share with other people. Solitary play is there from the beginning, and lives on in all of us — from suddenly tossing stones into a still pond to the subtlest dimensions of daydreaming to music. It can lead a child to the springs of its own creativity. But single play slips into second place for most of us for most of the time, and here again the father led one way into the surrounding world. He tended to introduce rules. 'I try and give him a little idea about how you score with the ball, and what counts and doesn't count. He doesn't always get it, but he's got the rough idea, I reckon.' Rules are the essence of games. Fortunately the English language makes this distinction between play and games. The French have to wrestle with one word, *jeu*, as the Germans do with *spiel*.

Almost all the active fathers saw the distinctions, sensed the changes. Play is pleasurable. Play can easily be solitary: one watches small children who play in parallel to each other, rather than together. Play is part of the child's animal growth: arching the back, kicking the legs, toddling, reaching, falling, climbing. 'Sometimes', said Marion, 'she gets up, goes a little way, not many steps I should say, and then bang! down on her bottom. You go quick, like, to pick her up, thinking she'll be crying, and she's not. She's chuckling and wants another go.' And play can be delightful in its utter pointlessness. That too might resurface later in adolescent high spirits, crazy humour, daft behaviour at weddings. But with these children I often felt that there was a hidden point. They were coming out of the den (womb, cot, utter dependence); and, if the father was there, he usually was signalling them on. For after 'play' he led them into 'game'. Children, as we know, play games intensely, and share and hand down a vast body of ritualized pleasure — Hide and Seek, Relievo, What's the Time, Mr Wolf?, Tin Can Tommy, Split the Kipper, counting games, Kiss Chase. The toddler who is now struggling at bedtime to communicate with father or mother in English — 'Whah Teddy . . . umpsch . . . mine . . . Teddy . . . whah . . . want' — will in a few score months be dancing around the school playground in a swirling gang, chanting 'Zig zag zolligar, zim zam bum' as he begins the new dip to start the next game. Everyone will understand the rules, as they will in later years when this sense of game and rule not only develops in adult sport and entertainment, but enters so many aspects of life, from law to war.

A second example where we can see, observe and record the father's relationship with the child in early years is language. During the first twelvemonth, the father seldom made very much of the baby's babbling. He could distinguish between a handful of noises, and clearly sense the difference between a baby playing with noises and one urgently seeking to communicate. This was partly because he usually spent so much less time with the child. The mother normally decoded the child's noises infinitely more subtly. But the father, if only during his bedtime visits, did have a part, and one which — if he had been given more information or time — he might have developed. As he rocked or stroked the child, he hummed with it (often very self-consciously if someone else was present). He blew out his cheeks and made odd noises in response to the baby: bear noises, ghost noises, bird noises and utterly indescribable noises. He smacked his lips, and made popping noises with his finger inside his cheek. I saw one father hold his hands up to the cotside lamp, with the baby on his lap, and throw shadows on the wall opposite. He didn't utter any English words but made lots of accompanying noises. What the plot of this mysterious theatrical was I never knew. But the little girl, her attention moving from his fingers to the wall to his mouth and back again, kept up a chorus in reply, and kicked her legs in delight.

Later the men often turned naturally to imitative, repetitive noises. If there was a pet around they did 'wuff wuff' or 'miaow miaow'. Out in the car for a quick spin they might turn to the baby seat in the back and say 'brmm brmm' as they revved up. Or point to 'moo moo' in the passing fields or 'quack quack' on the ponds. There was no self-consciousness about this. It was an agreed layer of tribal language. I am not sure that the child always linked the noise and the object. But even when they didn't they frequently liked the noise, and tried to imitate.

The change in the father's response came when the child began to use accepted language with a degree of confidence. When the child was very young several fathers bent over the baby and wondered 'What will her voice really be like?' And all except a declining group of 'traditional' or absentee fathers played at least a supplementary part during those baby-talk days. But now came a difference. The mother usually remained fairly tolerant of baby talk, and relatively (not always) patient of those passages of regression when the child retreated into earlier language, and started saying 'Me tired. Me sleep' when only last week he plainly said 'I'm sleepy' before curling up in the most awkward and uncomfortable of places under tables or at the bottom of stairs.

But the father was impatient for conversation and adult language. The child might be slow, hesitant, beginning a phrase six times over, and wandering away from the question asked. If the man was returning from the adult world of work, it could, just as with a working mother, sometimes be difficult to change gear and communicate at the child's pace and within the child's style. The difference was not that. It was an extra touch of frustration. The father wanted the child to be older in play and in language, for then he could be very much clearer what a dad might do. 'When he's about six or seven, I'll be able to show him things, teach him what not to do, point things out. He'll take an interest then.' Again, whether he fulfilled this in practice or not, the father saw himself as a beacon in the outside world.

With his ventures into play and language, the father brought another element: physical movement. Sometimes I witnessed a slightly irritable scene when a desperately organized mother had settled the baby in its bed, only for the man to arrive and insist on picking it up. After a yawn or squall or two, naturally it perked up and began to enjoy life. Having turned the 'on' switch and brought the baby to life, it could now be extremely difficult to find the 'off' switch, put it back to sleep — and go to that meal already hot for the table. Many a man was cursed for his thoughtlessness, but that doesn't really explain his consistent behaviour. The same often happened with toddlers and older children. They might not be docilely fast asleep. The mother had often engineered a gradual decrescendo: they were fed, changed, movement slowed, noise level dipping — a preparation for the end of the day. 'But you can wait up for Daddy. He'll be so pleased to see you.' Unfortunately Daddy often arrived like a sudden hurricane, picking the child up, whirling it round, ruining the rhythms of the early evening, fighting his way back into the forbidden lands of parenthood.

With an older child there was one clear instance where the father had indeed entered new territory. Perhaps ten of these new fathers carried their baby in a backpack. Even a generation or so back, for a man to walk around the shops trekking like an Indian squaw of old would have been unthinkable. For most it still was: the equivalent of men carrying handbags. But prams and pushchairs were a different story. The majority of these fathers had no hesitation in trundling one along in public. They openly enjoyed it. They played jokes — joggling, racing, turning corners on one wheel, stopping to point out familiar houses, a white cat on a red roof, spring branches waving in the wind. They met and talked without embarrassment with other men. 'If you'd asked my own father to take young 'un out in pram, he wouldn't just have said *no*; more than that. He'd have let them put him in jug, in chokey, first. Never saw a man do this in my father's day, and that's not so long since, is it?'

All these are novel entrances for the new male on the stage of ordinary childhood. What they offer for children is clear. For example, we have some evidence which suggests that the main plague of babyhood is not only colic or colds — but boredom. Babies are expected to sleep too long. Babies are endlessly laid on their backs. Sometimes this is in a confined unstimulating space (one father vowed not to have a fashionable cot with closed-in teak sides). Yet when the baby is picked up, and can use its eyes and ears and enjoy all the drives of curiosity, it becomes a changed creature — and we see a much more optimistic result. Similarly, the vivid impact of a father — even if it does disrupt the planned evening — can be a Technicolor even in a child's life. If it is hard to settle down again, that is partly because it has become just a bit more alive. And equally so with those backpack, pushchair and pram journeys — passive errands transformed into scenic tours.

If these are gains for the child, what of the father? For him, leaving aside for the moment the huge shadow of work (or of its untimely opposite, unemployment), he is clearly trying — however clumsily — to break into child care. Increasingly these fathers seem to want to display in action that this is not merely *her* baby, but *our* child. Yet, for a father to assert that it is *our* child, he almost always has to stake out a more primal claim — *my* child. As we orbit around this group of today's fathers, we can chart both his thrusts to escape from traditional roles, and the frustrations, mistakes and other defeats that he encounters. But in what sense is Amy or Ben *his* child?

Living along with and observing the fathers, it seemed possible at this stage to break the question down. To begin with, they all knew and felt they were the blood father ('That child's a part of me'). It is easy, in discussing new life styles, to overlook or underestimate this passion in the man. Perhaps, like the smoulderings beneath a silent volcano, it is there throughout life — and only bursts out in collision and crisis. Before, at, and just after birth, this sense of shared creation was plain to see. Then the daily round and the demands of work forced it back. Looking at men had uncovered something of fatherhood, even if much of it now retreated: whereas motherhood became, if anything, more salient. Next, the child gave the man a new status. Many of them talked about murmuring the word 'father', looking at themselves from the outside as in a dream. A personal as well as social identity was redefined. Whether this would be as true if the man knew he had not sired the child I do not know. That lies outside our scope.

Then he saw — and was rapidly made aware of — himself as economic provider. Again, whatever ideal or flexible arrangements may be publicly aired, it would be a mistake to underestimate this, for it was felt keenly: whether the man was unemployed or working;

whether he was a manual labourer or a desk-bound professional; whether the mother had a job or whether she did not. Whether he actually was such a potent provider comes behind the fact that this was how he felt his role — and with a sharpness not remotely sensed in childless days.

So far as I could tell, all these fathers bonded with their child, just as the mothers did. That does not mean that every one wholeheartedly wanted a baby ('Well, not yet really. But you do get older, and like Anne says, there comes a time . . .'). Not every one felt joy at the birth, or anything except a vacuum of feeling. Not all of them liked the look of the child ('I'd thought about him — or it might be her — but it didn't look like that. I'd imagined it . . . well . . . different'). There may sometimes have been streaks of rejection, but fundamentally they 'took to' the baby and surrendered themselves to the child.

The child is seeking it quite as strongly as the parent. The most intense, greedy, clinging relationship was with the mother. She was usually on the spot and supplied the demanded service. But from the earliest days it did not seem that there was a biological imperative to bond exclusively onto the mother. These babies might have bonded onto any care giver — grandparent, step-parent, brother, sister, aunt, uncle, foster parent, neighbour. Everyone in the world they had newly entered was a potential parent. What was required was availability and service, and even at a very young stage, the child, if it so arose, could tolerate and enjoy intense relationships.

So it seemed possible for the child to 'grow towards the father' in this sense too. But what happened was curiously different. The fathers who spent most time with the child in the first year were the twelve who were unemployed. In seven of these families the mother soon returned to part-time work to increase the household's income. Superficially these men were well placed to reverse roles and become the prime care givers. Though all of them *managed* the house and child fairly well, none of them became conspicuously nurturing fathers. The blockage was that they were with the child reluctantly, and they held on as strongly as they could to their old sense of identity — an identity defined by work. I never heard one of them primarily describe his job as 'being a father', in the unselfconscious way in which a woman freely spoke of herself to friends — 'I'm a mother now of course.' Motherhood was a job, fatherhood was not. Nor did I ever hear the word 'househusband'. Like many other terms which appear in magazines and books about the changing family, it simply was not part of the ordinary language through whose usage people perceive what they are.

Clearly length of exposure to the child was, by itself, not sufficient

to create the most vivid bonding. Yet that did coalesce for more
fathers than one might have expected, given the all-consuming claim
on time taken by their work. The type of father whom I described
at the birth as a 'sharer' seemed to make just that extra effort not
only to see the wide-awake child, but to use that time. Sometimes
these moments were spent in feeding: bottles and burps, and then
spooning up mushy food, and trying to get it into the baby's mouth
and not all over its nose, skimpy hair and wandering cheeks. But
mostly they were expended in play — not just half-hearted or
indifferent play (where he wearily picks up the toy every time the
child excitedly throws it out of the cot and pram), but concentrated
and mutual play. Once more it was the quality and not the quantity
of time offered to the child which seemed to deepen the relationship
on both sides.

The fathers whom in the hospital I had seen as a type that wholly
identified with the woman in labour now began to probe further.
Quite apart from play, they often took a larger part in feeding. Even
with breast-feeding, they might 'attend', and emotionally and in their
curiosity follow all its ups and downs, cries, interruptions, patches
of sleep, as closely as any mother. They might also be the one to
hear the baby's cry in the night, the first to come and pick it up,
as if they had a baby-tuned short-wave system in their ear.

Presence, food, comfort, play: perhaps that takes us closer to the
structure of the bond that these fathers made. Not that all of them
seemed to make much of a bond at all. It is difficult to make
judgements, but by the time the child was two some ten or a dozen
fathers had what, at best, might be described as an emotionally
neutral attitude and, at worst, a negative one. If they were later to
separate from the mother (and that was often clearly on the cards)
it looked very doubtful if they would miss the child all that much.
About half simply saw too little of the child during the early years
to have very much direct effect. This did not mean that they were
not concerned. Rob said to me: 'Didn't know there was all this much
to being a dad. There's a lot to it if you think about it. I never
rumbled that before. There's a lot more than seeing the missus has
enough money. We talk about Elaine a lot. In fact I wonder if it
isn't the *only* thing we talk about these days, even though I don't
see a lot of her in the week. When she's older and can stay up late,
that's when I'll enjoy her, I suppose.'

But lastly one should also note their *indirect* parenting. It is easy
to overlook the importance of the father at one remove. Many men
regularly came home to a sleeping child, and yet were excellent
fathers in another sense — not simply as providers but as stimulating
supporters of the mother. There was little doubt but that fathers who

could make this positive (and often sudden) switch from workplace to home, almost re-ordering priorities as they put the latchkey in the front door, play a striking part in lifting the morale of the new family. We know very little about indirect parenthood, and how those — whether men or women — caught in the vice of dominating work do have, or might realize, a full and rich part of childhood. It was not easy for most of them. The idea of changing your priorities as you cross the threshold, however well meant, was ultimately an illusion. Often they came home from the outside world, thinking in terms of decisions, plans, action. But what was sought, hoped, and sometimes clearly desired, was utterly different. It was to listen, to touch, to play, to share, to forget the ticking clocks.

A social scientist, falling back on the tablets of his own tribe, might describe that not as instrumental but as expressive. And, perhaps sometimes astonishingly, that is what many of these new fathers looked for, and sometimes achieved. For almost half of the fathers were strenuously trying to relate to the child in ways which, only a generation back, would have been just as real, but so much rarer. They did not always succeed, but what one noticed was the sheer effort. The child not only grew towards them — but was clearly beckoned. They wanted both a domestic, nurturing role and a public, providing one. They crossed their fingers and hoped the double desire was possible. Many a working mother has preceded them in this dilemma.

It is difficult to claim that they succeeded, but on the whole I thought they did. One test that I used was what happened when a two-year-old cried. Maybe she had fallen over and grazed her knee, or been scratched by a startled cat who wasn't in the mood for tail-pulling, or knocked her head on a sharp cupboard door. As in all these small disasters of childhood, she yelled and looked for comfort. In the first year she almost always turned to the mother, even if both parents were there. But by the second year it was more complex. She still usually targeted on the mother, because the mother was still usually there. But if — like the fathers in this last, active group — the man was around too, I could observe little difference. The child simply went towards the nearer, or the one who instinctively outstretched welcoming arms. In the encouraging environment, the small child bonds not with the mother, not with the father, but with both.

13
Androgyny and the
Imperatives of Work

In the *Metamorphoses*, Ovid tells the almost forgotten legend of the child of Hermes and Aphrodite. She was the love-princess from the sea. He became the god of dreams who led the way into the future. Their son was Hermaphroditus. Whilst bathing in the waters of Caria, he was seen by the nymph of the fountain of Salmacis, who instantly fell in love, and desired him. She asked the gods that the two of them might be made one body — in which all that was male and all that was female was then united.

The notion of the hermaphrodite is familiar to zoologists (the rudimentary ovary in the male toad) and to botanists (the stamens and pistils flourishing together in the double narcissus). But in psychology it has always been used in a sexual sense — in discussions of erotic relationships within one sex, bisexual behaviour, transvestism, and changing sex. Yet clearly the awareness of masculine and feminine which is emerging from this study of fathers is not that at all. Possibly that is why we need to use a different word from the vocabulary of the past: androgyny.

We usually know ourselves to be either man or woman, and later father or mother. There are mountains of psychological literature which report and measure what are termed characteristically male traits (aggressive, outward-looking, competitive, tough) and characteristically female traits (gentle, supportive, receptive, introspective). Though these distinctions are frequently, indeed usually, presented as truths about the human psyche, they are — as we see — often but mirrors held up to the prevailing culture. For what we are observing with these parents is by no means a confusion. It is an expression of a band of feelings that cannot efficiently be boxed in as masculine *or* feminine. They are simply, human; which is, perhaps, the point of the nymph's plea to the gods.

Many of the fathers here (and no doubt the mothers) transcend the traditional typing; and it has been claimed in current times that a quarter of women and a quarter of men display the accepted feelings or behaviour of the opposite sex, as well as those of their own. I would hesitate to rush into numbers: that way one is measuring the shifting mists. Yet this is still both a more accurate and more generous way of looking at the father's response than the traditional one. We have sometimes met men here mentioning what they saw as 'masculine' dimensions of their wife — 'She's never been what you might call a lovey-dovey type' — or wishing on a new-born daughter, as they named her, 'something that's a girl's name, but boyish'. But we have also picked up the fathers' own 'feminine' waveband. Like the man who said 'I found myself secretly touching.' It is the word 'secretly' which alerts you to a taboo being broken. Or Tom Arnold who broke down, buying blooms for his wife after they had just had twins — 'Made a bloody fool of myself at Interflora.' Another trespass across the borderline. This sense of a new or unfamiliar or unexpected stretch of feeling was all around most of these men. In those early, pregnant times: 'Just me and the baby in the dark'; the clumsy, half-stopped tears at birth; the sheer delight in the child — 'I touch her more than anyone else. More than Jacquie.' Touch, as so often, was the most eloquent signal of a language that, as yet, lay beyond ordinary words.

There was a generation of 'tender' men here, transmitting this broader spectrum of feeling to their child, but there was also a powerful phalanx of 'tough' men, who with equal intensity dispatched the traditional message across the generations. In looking at the new, we should not exaggerate its scale (whatever our views on its desirability) in a landscape long ago staked out by the old. In this study there is a sharp spotlight on men changing, but it would be wrong to overlook dominant contexts — psychological, cultural, economic — from which such fathers emerge. Even so fine a psychologist as Ian Suttie in *The Origins of Love and Hate* warns us that 'A man may take a condescending interest in children (under the guise of amusing them); but how many men can exhibit a real tenderness for babies?' Yet, if we leave the clinical couch, knock on doors, enter the family and listen to the male voice, the evidence is all around us.

If this is a new reality, we could set it out as a diagram. Suppose we split men into two groups: those who were either high or low in terms of expressing traditional 'masculine' or 'feminine' feeling. We can then do the same with women. If we now allow a degree of overlap ('androgyny') we could represent it like this:

FATHERS

	High Masculinity	Low Masculinity
High Femininity	Androgynous Father Androgynous Mother 1	Feminine Father Feminine Mother 3
MOTHERS **Low Femininity**	Masculine Father Masculine Mother 2	Father low on intensity of response Mother low on intensity of response 4

It may be necessary to underline that this is not a sexuality division, but a stylized way of setting out a father's or a mother's expression of feeling, towards a child or towards behaviour, which has traditionally been labelled as 'masculine' or 'feminine'. To emphasize the non-sexuality of this, one can take extreme points. There is no reason why a highly masculine or maybe lesbian mother cannot behave in an expressively feminine way with her child; and the reverse with a homosexual or bisexual father. It may be rare in practice; but in order to look at the concept of androgyny and to read many of the father's reactions we have to put aside sexuality. What we are looking at is opening up that wider range of legitimized human response to the child.

That said, only a small minority of these families could be confidently allocated to squares 2, 3 or 4. The *static* underlying pattern was of an expressively masculine father (part of square 2) and a feminine mother (part of square 3). But the *dynamic* trend was towards the duality in square 1: the increasingly androgynous parent. This is a fairly rough and ready approach, but it does help clarify the father's response.

We can take other bearings on these new fathers which may help us chart what we have met. For example, we could go beyond bonding, and consider what kind of masculine model they offered to their son or daughter. One active model in so many of these accounts was of the father who held keys to the wide, wide world, and of the mother who maintained the security of the hearth. Whether this is desirable or undesirable, one can only report that it was so even in dual-career families at one end or, at the other, ones in which the mother worked and the father was unemployed. So intense was the barrage of internal and external signals that this was the raw and basic balance. Next, and partly in consequence of the physical or psychological absence of the father, both son and daughter were usually growing up in a world of strongly visible female models. By contrast, the model that the father set his child was more mysterious. These fathers began with a pattern in which mother holds the child, father watches; mother is on the inside, father is spectator; mother brings up the child, father returns from work; mother passes the child on into the extended female environment of early schooling, father waits on the sidelines for later years. As we have observed, many men were trying — increasingly so — to break such patterns. But whilst they were one moment close, one moment distant to their child, the model they offered was frequently narrowly masculine. This was not always of their own choice and the mixed-up confusions of life are interesting. For example, many mentioned how irksome they found the thought of themselves being the bringer of discipline into the family. Frequently they recalled their own mother *threatening* them with the return of the father ('Wait till your dad gets home, I'll tell him and you'll catch it'), and vowed not to get trapped in that role. It was hard to escape. Similarly there was an expectation on the man to define the gender of the child — or, more usually, of the son. Soon after the child began to walk, it was the father who chivvied the boy out of 'sissiness', and simultaneously encouraged the 'tomboy' aspects of the girl.

There was also a touch of one kind of unreality about the father's model. It wasn't just that mothers gave their girls dolls and prams to play with. They gave them in a context. I was delighted to run into Janet outside the supermarket. She was pregnant again and stocking up well in advance. Her gleaming trolley was piled up with special-offer nappies, litre bottles of rosehip syrup or blackcurrant juice, endless cans of beans and soup. On top of all sat little Marilyn, whose birth I well remembered. Marilyn clutched a cuddly doll and (unusual in this sample) a dummy. So play merged into the continuum of life.

Contrast this with a call on Steve Campbell. When I first met him, he overwhelmed my questions with stories of rugby in the Welsh valleys. He had had a boy. The early evening that I knocked on the door, the child was being shown off to a long-lost aunt. He greeted me with relief, and we escaped from the cucumber sandwiches into the garden. 'Come and see what I've built, man.' It was a tree-house, perhaps the tiniest tree-house in the world, about thirty inches off the ground, and somewhat rough-hewn. We earnestly discussed whether he should lift tiny Derek into it, or whether — whilst he awaited the departure of the long-lost aunt — we might set about making a rope ladder. It was Tarzan-at-the-bottom-of-the-garden. Nothing in Steve's life involved tree-houses, swinging on ropes, lighting fires. There was a discontinuity between expected life and the male image. One notes this contrast between mother and father models dozens of times — fathers projecting a male fantasy, mothers projecting real life. Paradoxically that gave the man an extra dimension: he was the pilot who led to other possible worlds. Again and again, the clerical officer, the machinist, the dock worker, the dark-suited executive radiated this primordial sense of maleness — whatever their stated views about man, woman, child, family.

So, often in contradictory ways, the father displayed his tough self and his tender self, and passed on the image and the dilemma to the child. It must also be said that there is no necessary connection between androgyny and equality. Some of the men here who most extended their feelings after the birth of their first child were nevertheless quite hierarchical in attitude. Neverthless, if for the moment we put aside the more obvious markers, the androgynous father is already with us, if voiceless. The world of Tarzan and taboo was all around, but no one could live alongside these first-time fathers without frequently feeling their urge to develop tenderness as they had obviously developed toughness. It had its muddles and dissonance, and they sometimes looked back to their own fathers maybe with respect, maybe with love, but almost always across an emotional chasm. There was a sense of change — not dramatic, not a revolution in the ruins of the old. It was more like puzzled explorers entering a new landscape, worried about their supply lines but tempted by the next range of peaks. With the first child, the taboo on tenderness began to dissolve, not for all, but for enough for one to remark the change. And, looking at the enlarged love which so many of these fathers offered their child, I was reminded of a phrase of Susan Sontag in *Against Interpretation*: 'What is most beautiful in virile men is something feminine, what is most beautiful in feminine women is something masculine.'

Many men here, in their family lives, were often trying to discover or explore or express a gentler range of feeling than that to which their own father or grandfather seemed to admit. Obstacles stood in their way: most obvious, if not most deep or subtle, were the imperatives of work.

'By day, with even the children pent in schools, it is a village of women.' I often remembered that sentence from Phyllis McGinley's *The Province of the Heart* as I walked the streets to check some further bit of information about the family. Despite the fact that twice as many mothers now work than did so a decade ago, despite the rise in unemployment, despite shift work and flexible rostering, the daytime world is curious and alien territory to the active male. In *Toads Revisted* the poet Philip Larkin describes the sensation of leaving his office in the library for a stroll in the park:

> Walking around in the park
> Should feel better than work:
> The lake, the sunshine,
> The grass to lie on.

But the daylight realm is peopled with busy women, growing toddlers — and lost males, drifting, ill, killing time, expended. The poet, thinking of work as a toad, greedily returns to his office:

> Give me your arm, old toad
> Help me down Cemetery Road.

Once more we are not discussing what might be, or perhaps what should be, but what is so. The identity of the man comes substantially from his awareness of himself as a worker. Though a minority here would disagree, the overwhelming majority valued and ranked themselves in terms of the challenge, prestige, earning capacity or potentiality of their work. 'Labour', wrote Karl Marx, 'is external to the worker. It does not belong to his essential being. He does not affirm himself, but denies himself. His labour is merely a means to satisfy needs external to it. It is the loss of self.'

This is precisely what had happened with most of the fathers here, and why perhaps they felt both passionate and confused about their new child. They had not lost selfhood: they had found it, above all, in work, in being public. Just sometimes they found it in sport (their weekend brilliance at golf or football, almost always in all-male environments). But sport was, I began to think, more an extension of work than an extension of domestic living. The division between work and home still pushed man away from himself. External work sustained the home, and external work etched the outlines of the man's identity. His sense of significant living lay strongly there. This was as true of Mark Williamson, the docker, as of Piers Macdonald, the top civil servant. But the other, obverse or inner self searched for significance in private living. The birth of a first child was supremely that moment. It was not that this dimension of the man's being was atrophied, like the nipples on his hairy chest. I doubt if there has ever been a golden age when fathers like this fully and usually shared in the nurturing of their offspring, and expressed that sense.

This generation of fathers were pioneers. Many were marking out new dimensions of fatherhood possibly unknown to their own parents. Nevertheless, after the elusiveness of expressing feeling, which we looked at in the last section, this old toad — work — now crouched in their way. They had met him during the pregnancy months, some of them, when they became more keenly aware of the two worlds. They knew him at the time of birth, when they took either too little time off or quite the wrong time. They knew him after the birth when the initial glamour of the baby turned into another barrage of demands and, as we have seen, the emotional weather could be very unstable, with low bouts of depression all too frequent. Now came the hard days. It is a paradox of our society that the time when the father is most locked on to the child and begins to see fresh human vistas is the very moment when the old toad forces him back into his allotted place. The new father — if he worked — not only worked hard, but he very frequently worked much longer hours than other men or women. The absurdity of our social arrangements was crystal clear. Just as the father yearned to know the child better, so he found himself ever more absent from the home. This was for three reasons.

First, the birth often coincided with the stage when many were just building the foundations of a career: they had to guard their job on the factory floor, hold on at the office, go on that course, wait for that telephone call, attend that dinner, meet that man, land that extra job.

Second, as we saw earlier, first babies are surprisingly expensive additions. The needs (carrycot, pushchair, shoes, shoes, shoes) cry out for cash. And the bills tumble in. A long way from bachelor days, an aeon away from early married life. That means that the father seizes any chance of overtime. New fathers here often trebled that commitment. If overtime was not a possibility, there was everything from private consultancies (for people like Gerry and Robin who were in computers), to black economy moonlighting (like Ray, who ran a bar till midnight, sixty minutes after arriving home from his day in the bus shed). It was a treadmill: tired men with untaxed pound notes in their back pocket, chasing an ideal that they could never find.

Third, there was a fear that the sheer interrruption of birth jeopardized their position in the office or factory. Just to hold their own, they had to demonstrate time-consuming presence.

The bizarre position of the man became dramatically more clear as these children were born, taken home, welcomed into the world — and more of their fathers lost their jobs. The remaining fathers were shovelling away titanic mountains of public and paid work every hour they could grasp: the others mostly had vast oceans of time, but little skill in using it creatively within the family. Of course there were vivid exceptions. But this was the troubling norm. The young father in employment faced a point of maximum pressure on which all the drives and dynamics of work were focused. The young father not in employment was an economic castaway, marooned on his individual island.

Why don't men, who largely control both power and influence, object to this mismatch of public and private life? Is it fear of losing an old identity — what is often called, despite the evidence, 'the sturdy oak ideal'? Is it a reluctance to venture into deeper waters in search of the new, lest one ends wrecked on the rocks? Is it an instinct for relative safety and comfort and definition? Or is it simply not knowing what to do about societies which pile up economic questions in one corner, family questions in another, obscure one and then establish such byzantine and wasteful patterns that all either obey or despair?

It was not because fathers did not try. These chapters are studded with stories of men baffled by that attmept. But their section of the economic network gave them little choice. We have met them tough, and met them tender. Often the two qualities inhabited the same man. They met difficulties all around: from public opinion, from bureaucracy, from professionals, from their wives, from experts, from their workmates, from the nudging of their own psyche. Some difficulties (such as talking about their new role) were small; some (such as the absence of the male presence in childhood books) were merely passing ignorance; some (as with workmates) were thinly defensive; and others were jealous and territorial. But, behind all, still sat that old toad, work.

How then might society be loosened up so that men at least have the chance of a choice? In a technological world in which all too many men and women are pursuing a diminishing number of jobs, might it not be possible to open up possibilities of men playing an economic and a nurturing role? The most radical response to this question comes from Sweden. It is worth pondering.

Like so many fresh family policies, it was prompted by a falling birth rate. Sometimes this moves governments to increase child benefits (so as to encourage more babies) or improve nursery education (so as to release mothers into the work force); or, indeed, both. The Swedish approach was refreshingly original. There, the population increase in the 1970s was only 0·3 per cent and dropping. There was also a groundswell of women's rights, and new claims for equality between the sexes. In 1974, under the government of Olaf Palme as Prime Minister, a new law was introduced which gave a couple seven months' paid leave at the birth of the child. The mother and the father decided between themselves how to divide this up. Through a national insurance fund (largely financed by employers) they would usually receive 90 per cent of their normal income. They were also guaranteed the right to return to their jobs, without any loss of place, benefit or seniority. All legal arrangements were explicitly framed so as to be sexually neutral.

In the first year, two out of every hundred eligible fathers claimed this right. Most of those sought only a few days, and then went back to work. The government refined the programme, and amongst other details earmarked 45 days' leave for fathers (which they could transfer to the mother). Gradually the figure of claiming fathers rose to fourteen out of a hundred, though some of them only took one day, and half used less than a month of their legal allowance. There was a mild but real tendency for fathers with higher incomes either to seek no paternity leave at all or to ask for very little. We simply do not know whether the fathers who came home were later to play a closer part in the development of their young children.

Why was this? Certainly this was not a case of disadvantaged families. The more you earned, the less likely you were to claim the opportunity. Perhaps, despite the best efforts of the legislature, you did in fact lose opportunity, presence, long-range earning power. It has also been pointed out that, in a thriving 'black economy', a multitude of undeclared perks or payments on the side were lost as well. This may be so, but I would add a social dimension. Just as the captive housewife yearns for the busy traffic, relationships, excitements and gossips of that work world she has lost in order to become a mother, so the father is reluctant to leave that theatre to extend the part-time pleasures of home. He is only too aware of his own replaceability.

But the Swedes are, as ever, inventive and optimistic. The laws were changed to add on a 'special leave' of six weeks which either parent can take in the first seven years of the child's life. Even better, the special leave can be used in two-hour units in order to reduce the working day from eight to six hours, and so bring the parent sooner to the child. Of course, this also takes the pressure off the need for day nurseries and childminders. Added on to all this were fifteen days of leave a year to look after a sick child. The take-up there was much more striking.

Once again we come back to the economic and cultural

conundrum within which all fathers live. It is just within the bounds of acceptability to stay off work and look after a small girl with measles. It is outside the bounds of acceptability to stay off work to meet, enjoy and seal a relationship with a baby. The Swedish experiment (which deserves much more close research) seems to warn us on the side of caution: don't underestimate work.

Nevertheless, our structures of employment do have to change. This is partly because of the evolution of work itself (agrarian, industrial, services, technological) and partly because of the rise of structural unemployment, and the shortening of the dependence ratio, with the result that fewer and fewer active adults productively support an extensive tail of the young and the old. It is also partly because women assert their right to be part of that public workforce. In all, there could be infinitely more opportunities — flexitime, job sharing — for a more open approach to work, and a more generous entry into home. It would be wrong to overestimate the chance of sudden change. The quality of life — and a clear and extra degree of it that was in sight of these fathers — evolves more uncertainly.

14

Everyman

Most find it a puzzling exercise to fumble their way through the treacherous mists of memory to recall or discover what their fathers meant to them when they were young. A protective shutter comes down on our imperfect understanding, and we have little sense of how our parents' lives were in those faraway days. When we come to have our own child perhaps that shutter sometimes slides back a surprising degree ('Now I come to think of it, that's funny. Very funny. Because he delivered me'), and a mosaic of tiny details returns: but full fathom five thy father lies.

Mother is a much sharper memory from childhood. Though — even if she was always around and taking infinite trouble over breakfast, after breakfast, school, birthday treats, holidays, endless meals, clothes, money, illness, accident — she is for much of the time a big blurred recollection. Listening to men talk about their own fathers was often like looking through a hasty collection of party snaps: some hazy, some blank, some out of focus, some packed with people we can't quite remember, and a few so brilliantly immediate that they are fixed for ever at that passing moment. All parents have to accept that, though children may bulk large in our lives, we — like a ridge of hills enveloped in drifting cloud — can be ever *there*, but much more incuriously observed.

This study spotlights the man in the dense and sometimes obscure network of family relationships. Not because he is the most important, powerful or influential figure: though sometimes he is. And not because he can easily be plucked out of that landscape for solitary study. But because the male experience is astonishingly absent from our recorded knowledge, analysis, and policies for the family. Father remains the invisible man of our first chapter. We have tried to start from ordinariness. Many other fathers have far more dramatic experiences, of grief, handicap, separation, struggle, than those gathered on these pages. But perhaps this is a useful beginning for a dialogue that we should now open, just as we have long pursued the debates on motherhood and on the family.

Most men will become fathers. They will not receive all that much of a cultural bequest to help them in the art and science of the role: how dads become dads, and how they might emerge as better ones. The old strategies are changing. Except in some distinct regional and social groups, the aspiration towards becoming a 'traditional' father was so often melting away like the spring snow. By traditional I mean the man who unquestionably saw himself as the patriarch of his emerging family: authoritative, the bringer of discipline from outside. A second major strategy of fatherhood, that of 'the absent provider', was altogether more tenacious. As the supply of work shrank, and the supply of leisure expanded, there was still this phalanx of one-dimensional men. Many were under considerable financial strain, but sometimes they seemed to work twenty-four hours a day only for the reason that the good lord had forgotten to provide twenty-five. To the young family they could simply be that 'photo on the mantelpiece' or, as the French phrase has it, 'My father — he is a bank provided by nature'. But on every side, and despite the pressures against it, the third strategy — 'the nurturing father' — was steadily taking over new territories. So, standing back and looking at how this spectrum of emotional, cultural, intellectual, social, psychological and economic pressures are focused on the new father, it was broadly true that an old mix was weakening. As before, one must add a strong note of caution. The old mix was disappearing or vanquished: like a beleaguered army it had its social strongholds into which it could retreat, and left many (often surprising) pockets of psychological resistance behind. The fulcrum remained the overworked father, who, as we saw, felt maximum need and maximum alienation at the very moment he sought to make a period of joyous, creative and intimate life. But the new father, like the new child, was nevertheless finding his feet.

Yet not without great difficulty. With the declining size of the nuclear family, most had had little physical contact with very young children during their own adolescence. They had a brother or sister who was only two, three, four years younger than themselves. Babies — once so common in a household — were now unknown, highly delicate creatures — 'I'd rather run to the bus stop with a Ming vase under my arm, than pick up a baby. Mind you I expect I'd drop them both.' Ann Dalley in her study, *Inventing Motherhood*, muses: 'Men and children: the phrase sounds peculiar.' And she goes on to speculate: 'a whole generation of men has grown up who, unless they are involved professionally, have virtually no contact with, or experience of children other than their own. This cannot help them to be good fathers. It cannot be psychologically healthy for anyone.' This is a timely and persuasive point of view, though I am not sure that I am so absolute: history is forever embellished with the nostalgic myth of that lost golden age of the family. It was always there, yesterday. But what we are tracking here is much more about now, and tomorrow. Nevertheless, whatever the varieties and the intrinsic nature of modern family life — in which the normal can be abnormal — this is broadly what a lot of men know to be their experience, and yet not that of their own fathers or grandfathers.

That change could be met a little if on the school curriculum we found not only the three Rs but that most conspicuous of absent subjects of concern, education for future parenthood. As, over the last century, the balance for the responsibility of learning has tilted away from the family towards the school, this might surely (using the family as the centre, and not as the competition) be one of the great educational opportunities. In the humanities it would be hard indeed to conceive of a more potent one. But nothing, whether inside school or in less formal settings outside or after school, had made much of a contribution that was remembered by a single one of these fathers moving into the experience of parenthood. On the other hand they certainly had spent a number of years in class acquiring an impressive amount of irrelevant, frozen or impotent know-ledge.

The medical world was perhaps a degree more sensitive, but not much. The dearth of simple information or help for the future father was grotesque. We met fathers who did not know what a health visitor was (and wondered if somehow she had the right to take away the child if she judged the parents inadequate); and fathers who at a perfectly safe birth saw their loved wife electronically wired up (blip, blip, blip on the mini-screen), and thought they were suddenly in a life-or-death emergency. These fathers came from different social groups and had no reason before to be so involved with the health and medical services. They were not at all stupid (though, in the off-hand way of the moment, they could be treated as so). Basically, they were uninformed. And, though they surely carried a responsibility to learn, it was seldom made easy for them. The chief, often gnomic line of communication was between the professional service, veiled in strange verbal terminologies ('Uptake in epidurals is a facilitating factor, Mrs Romsey, with an elderly primigravida') and the passive woman ('Thank you so much, Doctor'). Sometimes the man never even reached that minimum. He might remain many degrees minus: 'I felt like the janitor, not the father.'

Men were asking for information about birth, childhood and parenthood. Fathers of teenagers were in the same situation. What did the man do if the daughter dyed her hair green, or the son got hold of a lethal motorbike as soon as he legally could? What happened if a youngster looked like abandoning education, or dropping out of mainstream society, or sank into the apathy of pointless, caged-in education and apparently endless unemployment? How long should the leading-rein be, and when and how did the father let go? Once upon a time it may have seemed clearer: twenty-one, the key of the door, or later giving away the bride before the altar. So fathers with eighteen years' experience behind them were often not all that different from new fathers in their sense of forever entering a fresh stage of their lives with not much more than their own wits, common sense and instinct to see them through. Rex Sykes, a rather battered city commuter, said: 'My first kid was really like a prototype. If he'd been a sketch on the design board instead of the old twinkle in the eye, we'd never have built it. We'd have wanted tests, models, pilot runs. But with a child, you don't have the options. Trouble is, now he's a young lad, doesn't seem to take after me at all, and it's all just the same. I got better with my daughter, but not that much better, and who knows what's next with her? Perhaps by the time I learn to be a father I'll be a grandad.'

In previous chapters we have observed the lack of elementary information on birth which could help the man to play a more active part, and more easily bond into the basic family of mother, child and father. It cannot be difficult to organize antenatal classes in a style, place and time which would attract and hold more men. In some cases where there are enlightened employers with a large workforce, they could best be held not only in hospitals but in the factory too. Sometimes it might be possible to introduce some element of handling or observing real children. But certainly simulation with models of a baby is straightforward, even if one is only explaining how to hold, how to bath, change a nappy, or wrap up at the right temperature. Neither can one see any reason why practical literature cannot be prepared which sets out the twenty things which need to be seen to (from transport to having telephone coins in his pocket) immediately before birth. And if we are to have high technology birth, with its scans and monitors and no doubt much more to come, that too needs explaining both alive and in literature.

The scope for the educational and health services is huge, though it may well be that the media, television, books, radio, and magazines take the most influential initiatives as they so often have before in helping change parenthood. A whole pacakage for fathers is needed. One should not expect overnight changes (as some Swedes did with the introduction of their paternity leave) but no doubt many fathers would become more supporting to the mother and more caring to the child if the frontiers of ignorance were pushed back a degree or so. And a few fathers, without their present lack of confidence and lack of data, might be a shade less overpossessive about their wife and less critical of any professional aid she and he received.

We have touched on the changes in family structure which are, in part, causing shifts in man's sense of himself as father. But other ones are playing a part too. The increase in the use of efficient contraception has given woman a greater control of her body, and for both man and woman the chance of planned instead of fortuitous parenthood. And the shift from home to hospital birth has been equally dramatic, though infinitely less well thought out. Parents sometimes think too little consideration has been given to their views and their wishes (in anything from home confinement, the physical posture in which to give birth, the timing of discharge from hospital). Hard questions by them had, they felt, been muffled away either by medical orthodoxy or by vague claims about 'reasons of medical safety'. But high-technology birth is here. I have reported that in the fifty years between 1920 and 1970, the proportion of first-time babies born at home dropped from 80 per cent to 1 per cent. It is a colossal drop. Home birth did not necessarily mean that the father was there. We do not have all that much hard evidence on this, but if we consult the excellent work of John and Elizabeth Newson we can see that in their survey of 700 births in Nottingham in the late 1950s 13 per cent were attended by the father (15 per cent had a woman relation present, and another 15 per cent had a neighbour there). At *none* of their hospital births was the man there.

After some time experience has changed — rapidly too. Gone is the next-door neighbour, or the woman in the street who made a reputation as an informal midwife. Gone is mother, sister, auntie, cousin. But father is a-coming in. This revolution has taken not fifty years, but ten: from effective zero to over 80 per cent. It is of a piece with the increasing rapidity of many other changes in a post-industrial or technological society. And yet that change is not quite all it seems. Ancient attitudes are uncritically allowed to creep into and sometimes dominate modern practice. Many a man is physically present at a hospital birth, and yet is psychologically kept at the bottom of the stairs, metaphorically putting the kettle on, awaiting the first scream and the official announcement. Similarly the whole support system, which at one moment is bewilderingly complex, is suddenly withdrawn; and two young parents in one of those rows of nesting boxes which we call suburbs or housing estates are largely left to the most demanding and significant phase of all: how to bring up a young child. If we did no more than develop the role of the health visitor into an education and health worker (as likely to be a man as a woman) with adequate resources and training for a penetrating community role, that would be something. But more is needed, and it may demand a good deal of self-help, with parent groups springing up and sharing experience and need. Amongst them, perhaps there could be some father-to-father ones, discussing the problems that affect them. And amongst those (as employed mothers have also learned) there is no bigger one than our old companion work itself.

There lies the stone-age rock blocking many a father's search for fresh ways back into the family. Work can be hard financial necessity. But even if there is lots of money around, and the extra hours are simply converted into figures in a black bank account, it almost wholly monopolizes the lives of some men, the workaholics. For work is also about status and ranking, and it breeds a large complex world of its own from which the family might be the first to be excluded. Who hasn't met older children, long supported by the man's efforts, who could not construct a sentence to explain what their father did? Work too was rigid. You either had it or you did not; and it came in large clean-cut blocks. Against this, notions of job-sharing, flexitime, role reversal, time-sharing, were as yet mere drill-holes in the rock. To blast that open would still require great shifts in how we saw and ordered the world. For time was abundant and work was scarce. Increasingly, and without planning, we were heading for a society where there was hardly any work for people under the age of twenty. They were kept in school, and when progressive rises in the leaving age (from 12 to 16) no longer were acceptable, and when compulsory military service (from 18 to 21) ended, as did the big expansions of further and higher education (from 16 to 23), society was left consoling the young with unemployment training schemes — or simply handing out survival cash. With mature people there is increasing pressure to reduce the real retirement age from 65 or 60 to a point in the fifties whilst life expectation moves upwards in the seventies. And those who lose their positions in mid-life discover it extraordinarily hard to get back inside the world of outside work for those brief remaining years. All this focuses maximum pressure on the modern family at its most vulnerable point.

There are of course diverse patterns. But consider a common and vivid one. From birth to twenty-one, men are economically largely unproductive. Leave this gap vacant for now. From fifty-five, there is a compulsory (the job goes) or alluring (prospect of that silver handshake or taking that pension) falling away from the working force, and the entry to an increased lifespan. Go back to the gap. From twenty-one to twenty-six the man helps assemble the launch-pad for a new family. The first baby comes for him (maybe the mother is two years younger) at about twenty-six or twenty-seven. The second baby (in Britain, but not in all countries) is spaced about two years after. If there is a third child (and having two girls or two boys may tempt parents to try for one of the other sex), the spacing now would most likely be about three years. This takes the father up to the age of about thirty-three or thirty-four when he helps complete his family. It may remain intact, or he may go and start another one (divorce alone has increased by 400 per cent over twenty years, separation even more) — in which case all these pressures are not doubled, but trebled or quadrupled. But suppose the marriage does remain stable and lasting, and not hit by any thunderbolts: then he has about twenty years to help set his children on the road to future parenthood, and another twenty years in which — unless he is very successful, independent, as eminent as a judge or wholly obscure — his departure from the workforce normally looms up. He may brush the thought away, and there are infinite combinations of the weave — but the central motif in the pattern is that the world of the growing child and the father's allegiance or captivity to his world of work are an almost perfect chronological match. Yet, starting with a blank drawing board, would we have designed society that way? And need we accept that momentum, which forever pushes and locks those two pieces more tightly together?

If work could be more loosely organized or shared, then many urgent questions would take on a new and more optimistic colouring. In times when almost everyone, including the small child, was pulled into the workforce — man, woman and child in field or factory — the aim was to use the shelter of custom or deference or the church to gain holidays, festivals, fun time or family time, off work. By 1950, as retirement was accepted, weekends becoming sacred, and the eight-hour day coming in, headteachers were setting pupils (held in school by the rising school leaving age) essays or discussions on 'the problem of leisure'. By 1980, with the microchip revolution taking over they — like everyone else — were talking about 'the problem of unemployment' in what is, after all, one of the most affluent and wonderfully equipped societies that man has ever known. All particular questions such as paternity leave or work-sharing are embedded in that pattern.

Whether human emotion rises from such social patterns, or whether its springs run more deeply and, in origin, rise independently, is a question to pursue elsewhere. But certainly if we dot in the emotional outline of the father it is quite different from that of the mother. There is his frequently narrow line back to his own father ('Sometimes we feel closest when we're silent'). Until critical moments erupted, and passion emerged volcanically from underground, communication might be stylized, a string of expected phrases and gestures; laconic.

Man spoke to man about such intimate matters as childhood and family life often like passing ships communicating by semaphore or flag signal. Money, sport, or politics were far more open subjects.

The father was circumscribed by all these powers — the woman, the professional, work, inexperience, the enveloping culture outside him and the inherited culture settled deep in his personality. Fatherhood did not always prove to be what he had imagined in the night or in daydream. It burst with surprises, bombshells, fireworks, and continued spectacularly to do so. That it yielded such an abundance of joys, and ('Well, you just live on and on inside your kid, don't you? When we're gone, well, he'll remember a bit of us — hope it's the right bit — and pass that on to the grandkids') a sense of that fundamental human investment which enriches life with so much of its meaning, is a tribute to many a man's wit in what Joseph Conrad called the 'art of intricate navigation' in unknown waters.

Some of this is new to our own times, and points towards tomorrow. Some has been there since father was a hunter. The traditional role of absentee provider lives now as it did then. So does his first confidence in *doing* rather than in *being*. External discipline for the child and unquestioned authority at the ceremonial meal table may be vastly weakened and muted into consultation. But the traditional father is still with us.

Perhaps it is the new father we might ponder. He is gradually pushing out from his minority position, winning waverers, eroding the old. Closer to the child; physically and psychologically more present — when possible — within the full family; curious about the boy or girl's growth; engaged on the eternal quest for significance inwardly as well as outwardly; having the same confidence in being that the traditional father had in doing. That man — or parts of him — is everywhere in these interviews.

But can he ever be that equally nurturant father who matches the caring mother in a world where both have a freedom of work and of home — a joint freedom that does not threaten or diminish the child's right to be a child? Even more problematical is the emergence of the nurturing fathers developed from that ultimate envy of the female: his biological inability to give birth to a child, or to summon milk. And do such matters lie beneath his doubts — once he transcends the traditional role — of being a first-class father in a style unknown to his ancestors? As the psychologist Ian Suttie put it:

'It is clear that at all times the male has a natural drive to usurp maternal functions and so to redress the unfairness of evolution in this respect. Further, any immaturity in his own character will intensify his nurtural-tenderness-jealousy of his child's relationship of his own wife (his mother). On the one hand therefore he tends to displace the mother vis-à-vis the baby; on the other to displace the baby with the mother. Like the child he seeks the undivided attentions of each.'

The experience of fatherhood is 'a continuous excursion', and can be followed with a great deal of fascination and respect. Even in pregnancy and at birth, these men had a more intimate part than at first seemed obvious in what they accepted as 'being principally a female miracle'. But that was just the start of fatherhood.

15

Conclusion

At the beginning of this study, we circled around some preliminary questions. Was there some shift afoot in modern fatherhood? Had we become so exclusively concerned with the bond between mother and child that we neglected what the father might offer, the possibility of a double dynamo behind the child. Were varieties of traditional fatherhood emerging in Western societies — fresh nuances and relationships which each man sought out for himself? In the private world of the family, did men now want to offer their child something different from what they remembered of their own fathering? Why did we know so little of fathers, and how was it that they were one of the lesser-observed species?

The evidence behind this extended essay was drawn partly from what literature we had. It came from a national survey of almost 12,000 fathers interviewed when their children reached the age of five. It came from a hundred men who were entering fatherhood for the first time. It claims no more than to be a starting-point for what must become, in part, a speculative essay. We have lived it through, and not only the answers but the questions too have changed. As so often, at the end of inquiry, one would like to go back to the start and ask the questions over again. They would sometimes be different, and differently ordered: but the decision to be as receptive as possible was probably the right one at this time. A finer honing would now be needed. Many questions that now seem obvious were hidden, unthought of, or differently angled at the beginning. A lot of them are practical. One is the need for serious and central education for future parenthood in schools — not an easy argument to advance. Its weak spots are immediately exposed. Why should the state rather than the family or the community claim this role? And how are teachers equipped to become high priests of parenthood? After all, as one cynic said to me, 'If we'd left it to teachers to teach us to talk, a lot of us would belong to the silent minority.' A painful punch: but nothing I met here convinced me that fathers would become better fathers simply by leaving all to nature and custom. If they were changing, and there was little doubt that this was often so, then it was mostly prompted by the media — television, baby books, radio programmes, magazines — though often at one remove, through friends or through the woman. The communications network has to have delicate antennae in order to survive. It picks up the rhythms, shifts and crises in life. In return, it enjoys influence rather than power. Yet it seemed a pity that the great state near-monopolies in education and in medicine were so unresponsive and slow-moving in comparison. A strong approach to coming parenthood can no longer be left to the elders of the tribe, or to grandma round the corner. Both are scattered or gone; and the necessary knowledge is often new. Wise old saws only lead one first step along the way to understanding and helping a child today. So, whatever the weaker points in the argument, it could be right to seek means by which boys can be introduced to the prospect of fatherhood during their organized schooldays. If they did little more than cradle a live baby, tell a story, or join a playgroup, and then talk about it, they would nevertheless have an advantage that none or few of these fathers enjoyed. But of course it could be far more developed than that. Doubtless this would not work miracles of information: usually we only reach for urgent knowledge in a crisis and not before one. 'Preparation for . . . ' is not so attractive. Yet it does seem a waste that having created a vast and complex education system which, to a significant extent, displaces the family we have still not found ways of injecting mature family knowledge into schooling. Education for parenthood could be somewhere on that curriculum: it would, if only modestly, have helped almost every father here.

There also emerges a case for the health and medical professions to take much more note of the man. Clearly there have been considerable advances, which we have, as yet, hardly assessed. The most conspicuous has been the arrival of the man at the hospital birth. This varies from region to region, but overall we seem to be looking at a rise, over only ten years, from 1 per cent attendance to 80 per cent being present — the pioneer generation.

Again it is sometimes a matter of getting the nuts and bolts right. Several were missing here. One was antenatal preparation. Only the most concerned men went to such classes, and this was because — in time, place and content — they may be conceived wholly within the perspectives of motherhood. Times would have to be altered so that the father actually had a chance of attending: the coffee-morning approach is hardly relevant to a working man. With place, one might hope that trade unions would ask large employers for facilities in the factory or the office block. This would only meet the needs of some men, perhaps a fifth, but it would be a significant step to take concern for the future baby inside the workplace. The men would be more available, perhaps have more confidence on their own territory; maybe the unions would to some extent commit themselves further to the family, and — if only very little — the boundaries and barriers between fathers' double world of home and work would have been crossed. Antenatal classes within clinics and hospitals also need a fresh look, so as to attract and inform the father. I took the simple example of no father being offered a stethoscope to hear his unborn child's heartbeat, then the lengths to which some went to find some other instrument ('I've been trying with the beer glass on Liz's belly'); and the curiosity with which men viewed — too late — the hospital technology of safe birth. It is not that these are ends in themselves, but they are inviting starting-points from which the immediate practical needs (transport, coins in the pocket for the telephone) can be developed, followed by discussion of feelings and of the needs of the mother and the child. Not that this would bring all the fathers flocking, but a good many could be won over to a keener or more open concern, just as they have with their presence at the birth itself.

     But behind these mechanics subtler questions lurk. One is the attitude of the medical and health professions towards fathers. This may only be one extension of their general approach to their clients, but, as I listened to fathers all over the country, it seemed that they particularly felt that they were too often treated as hindering objects rather than people, and, more especially, as fathers: ('The paediatricians were explaining it all — not to me — but to these visiting American doctors'). To an extent this can be understood, since in the pace of pregnancy, birth and early childhood the priority had to be the mother and child. It was also true that many of the doctors, midwives, nurses, health visitors had not experienced parenthood themselves. But that hardly explained the narrowness of perception, because ultimately it was not personal at all, but cultural. It could only be countered not by protest and complaint ('I could have nutted her'), but by education and discussion. A serious concern and interest in fatherhood and the male experience should be an essential part of any basic training in health, nursing and medicine.

     Perhaps too we might see the question of fatherhood as part of men's arrival in early childhood. For it is not only within the family that many fathers seem to be seeking a closer relationship. This is taking place in law where more men seek the custody of their small child, if the marriage breaks up, and are prepared to lose the public world in order to bring up the boy or girl themselves. The odds may still be stacked against them, but a new current is flowing. It is taking place in voluntary work. One can come across men acting as childminders or playgroup workers and very often — almost like the first cuckoo in spring — a woman will tell precisely when the first man arrived on her scene. Their numbers are small and their arrival very recent, but they are there. It is happening in the professions: we have the first group of male midwives, only a score or so as yet; more men applying for posts in nurseries or infant schools — again, not many, but again a distinct memory of when the man first appeared. If you walk the shopping precincts or stand outside the school gates, you see a changing image: men pushing prams, carrying babies in backpacks, holding hands with children, taking them and collecting them. Much of this would have been unthinkable to many of their own fathers, even a matter of public shame.

Yet this could be viewed with unease by women. It carries not only the possibility of more sharing relationships, but also a latent threat. Men enjoy control of the commanding heights as far as the eye can range: they stand on the moon and look at planet earth. But one perpetual territory traditionally belongs to the woman — birth and early childhood. Does a concern with an extending male sensibility, a new staking-out of rights, mean that this will be invaded too? I suspect it does, but am doubtful whether even if we slept through a generation we would wake up and find ourselves in some unfamiliar topsy-turvy land, in which the balance between the sexes had quite altered. I also doubt whether a new school of inquiry into fatherhood as an institution and as an experience will change the prevailing bias in our study of the family. But it should help. There is no sense of a male backlash here (much recent work on fathers has been done by women). But radical change, if desired, would need more than this. The new father has to be seen in context.

The family remains a highly conservative institution, especially so at its most intense moments — marriage, birth, crisis, success, death. It evolves with caution, and that makes the present record more remarkable; for it is clearly a little special to travel amongst one of the first generations of what could become a broader and different style of fatherhood. How much of that promise will be realized is not certain, and one is inclined to expect modest rather than spectacular change. For we have seen something of the cultural and

institutional barriers that can stand between the father's inner self and
his public expression. There are the expectations directed at him (not
least by women): the driving demands of work, and the way it has
become entwined with his identity, his very sense of who he is. There
is his lack of knowledge and the distant attitude of the professionals.
But something has been achieved which mirrors what many mothers
too have achieved. This inquiry started from a concern with working
mothers. Some 6 per cent of mothers with a child under five went out
to work. They did not always want to, but they usually welcomed it
and often fought for it. All the evidence is that if there were more
alternative care for small children this figure would rise, though, even
with flexible choice, it would still be a minority. In Chapter 2 we saw
that if the state or private bodies provided only a minimum of such
care, it was the father who most frequently offered the supplementary
and flexible addition — which often helped another fifth of mothers to
work part-time. In Chapter 13 we stood this question on its head, and
analysed how many fathers might choose to stay at home with a child
if there was paternity leave. Our most solid example was the Swedish
scheme, and broadly 10 per cent of men were taking up part of the
option. No full and free choice is yet possible for either the woman who
wants to work or the father who wants to be more at home with his very
young child. Doubtless, in an imperfect world, it may never be so.
Mother at home with the young child and father out seeking provisions
is overwhelmingly what happens, and how people see motherhood and
fatherhood. What we are logging here is something different. It is a
shifting of the external and inner boundaries, a small but very
important movement in how those lines are drawn: an extension of
options. Only a few mothers may wish to work when they have a
young child, only a few fathers may wish to be at home. It could be
right for them and their child; but they also send out ripples which have
an effect on everyone else. That is what we have seen.

Yet the most delicate and important questions were not about social
mechanics (such as education for parenthood or better strategies by the
medical professions), nor yet about choices and chances (men in early
childhood posts, mothers in employment, paternity leave). They were
about male sensibility when the child entered his world. I often found
that I was one of the few people, sometimes the only one, to whom the
man had spoken his feelings. He may not have done this with the
woman ('I never knew you thought *that*' was a common interjection
in the interviews), perhaps because she excluded him, or did not expect
it of him or was obviously much better at such discussion herself. He
hardly ever explored his private response with male colleagues at work.
Conversation there was ritual, stylized, public — wages, sport,
weather, holidays, politics, the job in hand ('my mates just didn't want

to know', 'Don't know whether they were bored or embarrassed, may
be just plain not interested').

I doubt if that was wholly so. Women inherit a culture which enables
them to express intimate feelings. The mothers talk openly, freely and
at length, between themselves about the minutiae and sensation of
parenthood. Not every woman will use this chance, but nevertheless
it is there, and the mothers are far more practised, skilled and confident
than the men in discussing and sharing the delights and depressions of
parenthood. This does not mean that the fathers care or feel any less.
They are anxious to express fatherhood. But they often met dilemmas.
One was their lack of practice in articulating the gentler feelings,
whether in word, touch or action. Sometimes they put up defences:
perhaps that was what was happening when Steve Campbell countered
my baby questions with rugger reminiscences or when John Callaghan
coped with his emotion ('a drip feed of roses') by a Stone Age reaction
('the hand you need to grab a spear or axe'). It was there too in shyness
and uncertainty in handling the child. The first-time father needed a
new vocabulary of expression if he was to attune his private with his
public self. Perhaps the mothers, sharing intimate life, had always
known this of him: voiceless love in the dark. But for these men it was
the entry into fatherhood that so often stirred such deep feeling, along
with a touch of frustration (though Carmen said, 'My man, he just
makes this great choice of notes'). The tap-roots of fatherhood run
deep. The image I take away is of men in tears at the birth, and yet
feeling they had to disguise them. The question I most remember asking
is 'When did you last cry?', knowing that so often it would be countered
with 'Not since I was a child myself'. To release the full force of
fatherhood will mean breaking the masculine taboo on tenderness.

Bibliography

Aries, P. *Centuries of Childhood* (Jonathan Cape, 1962).

Arnstein H. S. 'The crisis of becoming a father' in *Sexual Behaviour*, April 1972.

Barber, D. *Unmarried Fathers* (Hutchinson, 1975).

Benedeck, T. 'Fatherhood and Providing' in Anthony, E. J. and Benedeck, T. (eds) *Parenthood — Its Psychology and Psychopathology* (Little and Brown, Boston, 1970).

Benson, L. *Fatherhood: a sociological perspective* (Random House, 1968).

Bigner, J. 'Fathering, research and practice implications' in *Family Co-ordinator* (October, 1970).

Biller, H. 'Father absence and the personality development of the young child' in *Developmental Psychology*, 1970.

Biller, H. *Father, Child and Sex Role* (Heath, Lexington, 1971).

Biller, H. and Meredith, D. *Father Power* (McKay, New York, 1974).

Bittman, S. and Zalk, S. *Expectant Fathers* (Hawthorn Books, 260 Madison Avenue, New York 10016, 1978).

Blood, R. O. and Wolfe, O. M. *Husbands and Wives* (Free Press, 1960).

Bradley, R. A. 'Fathers' presence in the Delivery Room' in *Psychosomatics*, November-December, 1962.

Breen, D. *The Birth of a First Child* (Tavistock, 1975).

Bronfenbrenner, U. *Two Worlds of Childhood*.

Brown, G. W. and Harris, T. *Social Origins of Depression* (Tavistock, London, 1978).

Corbin, M. (ed.) *The Couple* (Penguin, London, 1978).

Cronenwett, L. R. and Newmark, L. L. 'Fathers response to childbirth' in *Nursing Research*, 1974, 23, 2, 210–217.

Curtis, J. L. 'A psychiatric study of 55 expectant fathers' in *US Armed Forces Medical Journal*, No. 6, 1955.

Daley, E. A. *Father Feelings* (Wm. Morrow and Co. New York, 1978).

De Frain, J. D. 'Fathers Guide to Parent Guides: review and assessment of the paternal role as conceived in popular literature' 1974 Annual Meeting, American Association of Marriage and Family Counsellors.

Dockrell, W. B. and Hamilton, D. (eds) *Rethinking Educational Research* (Hodder and Stoughton, 1980).

Dodson, F. *How to Father* (W. H. Allen, 1974).

Fein, R. A. 'Men's experiences before and after the birth of a first child' phD thesis, Cambridge, Mass., 1974.

138   FATHERHOOD

Fein, R. A. 'Men and Young Children' in Pleck, J. and Sawyer, J. (eds) Men and Masculinity (Prentice Hall, 1974).

Green, M. *Goodbye Father* (Routledge, 1976).

Hestad, G. O. and Fayan, M. A. 'Patterns of fathering in the middle years' *Proceedings* National Council on Family Relations (St Louis, 1974).

Howells, J. G. 'Fathering' in Howells, J. G. (ed.) *Modern Perspectives in International Child Psychiatry* (Oliver and Boyd, 1969).

Howells, J. G. 'Fallacies in child care: that fathering is unimportant' *Acta Paedopsychiatrica*, Vol. 37, nos. 3–4 (1970).

Jessner, L., Weigert, E., Foy, J. L. 'The development of parental attitudes during pregnancy' in Anthony, E. J. and Benedeck, T. (eds) *Parenthood* (Little and Brown, 1970).

Kahan *The Expectant Father's Survival Kit* (Monarch, 1230 Sixth Avenue, New York, 10020, 1978).

Kitzinger, S. *Giving Birth: The Parents' Emotions in Childbirth* (Gollancz, 1971).

Kitzinger, S. 'Pregnancy — Time of Opportunity in Marriage' in *Marriage Guidance*, May 1970, vol. 12, no. 3 (National Marriage Guidance Council).

Kitzinger, S. 'Sex before and after birth' in *Midwife and Health Visitor*, Sept. 1972, vol. 8.

Kitzinger, S. 'Pain in Childbirth' in *Journal of Medical Ethics*, vol. 4, no. 3, Sept. 1978.

Leach, P. *Who Cares?* (Penguin, 1979).

Levine, J. *Who will raise the children? New options for Fathers* (Lippincott, 1976).

Love, L. R. and Kaswan, J. W. *Troubled Children: Their Families, Schools and Treatments* (New York, John Wiley, 1974).

Lynn, D. B. *The Father: His Role in Child Development* (Brookes Cole, 1970).

Maddox, B. *The Half-Parent* (Deutsch, 1975).

Martin, M. *Teach yourself Mothercraft* (English Universities Press, 1950).

Mayle, P. *How to be a Pregnant Father* (Macmillan, 1980).

Mednick, B. R. 'Intellectual and behavioural functioning of 10-12 year old children who showed certain transient symptoms in the neonatal period' in *Child Development*, 1977, 48, 3, 844–853.

Millar, T. P. 'How to get father to help discipline kids' in *Chatelaine*, August 1973.

Newson, J. and Newson, E. *Toys and Playthings* (Penguin, 1979).

Oakley, A. *Becoming a Mother* (Martin Robertson, Oxford, 1979).

Oakley, A. *Women Confined* (Martin Robertson, Oxford, 1980).

Piachaud, D. *The Cost of a Child* (Child Poverty Action Group, Pamphlet 43, 1979).

Pieck, J. H. 'Men's roles in the family' in *Sex Roles in Sociology*, (Proceedings, Merrill-Palmer Institute, Detroit, 1975).

Pollack, M. *Nine Years Old* (M. T. P., Lancaster, 1980).

Provence, S., Naylor, A. and Patterson, J. *The Challenge of Day Care* (Yale University Press, 1977). Has one footnote on fathers, even though they

are the major providers of day care, when mother works, in the
community.

Rapoport, R. and R. N. and Strelitz, Z. *Fathers, Mothers and Others*
(Routledge, 1977).

Rapoport, R. and Rapoport, R. *Working Couples* (Routledge, 1978).

Richards, M. P. M. (ed.) *The Integration of a Child into a Social World*
(Cambridge University Press, 1974).

Senn, M. J. E. and Hartford, C. (eds) *The Firstborn: Experiences of Eight
American Families* (Harvard University Press, 1968).

Stafford, L. M. *One Man's Family: A Single Father and his Children*
(Random House, New York, 1978).

Schaffer, R. *Mothering* (Fontana, 1977).

Turner, C. *Family and Kinship in Modern Britain* (Routledge, 1969).

Valentine, C. W. *The Normal Child* (Penguin, 1962).

White, B. L., Kaban, B. T., Attanucci, J. S. *The Origins of Human
Competence:* the final report of the Harvard Pre-School Project.
(Lexington Books, Lexington, Mass, 1979).

The *Brian Jackson Memorial Trust for Children* has been set up to identify and promote new and imaginative ideas aimed at helping children achieve their full potential and to live happier and more satisfying lives with their families. The Trust is particularly concerned to support innovatory projects designed to improve the quality of family life. It will also publish a biennial handbook full of facts, statistics, research and commentary on children and everything that affects them.

If you would like to see the ideas in this book carried forward please send a donation to

> The Honorary Treasurer
> Brian Jackson Memorial Trust for Children
> National Extension College
> Brooklands Avenue
> Cambridge CB2 2HN

who will also send further information on request.

Index

Agpar score 70–1
androgyny 111–20
animal behaviour research, and the
   biological imperative 11–12, 13

babies
   boredom 107
   crying 91–2
   father's fascination with 89–90
   feeding 90–1
   holding positions 71–2
   physical contact with fathers 106–7
'baby blues' 94
baby talk 73, 105
biological imperative, and motherhood
   11–13
birth
   father's presence 16, 58–9, 68
   father's reactions 68–72, 73, 74–6
   home confinements 77, 125
   ignorance of 52, 123
   refusal to attend 73–4, 75
   see also British Births Survey
bonding 13–14, 78–9, 90, 108–9
Bowlby J. 11
British Births Survey 21–3
brooding *see* couvade
Butler N. 6, 21, 22

Canada, home births 77
childminding, and working mothers 24–5
children
   contact time with fathers 25–6
   financial cost 49, 50
   importance of male first-born 83–4
   naming 81–3
   see also babies
contraception 40, 125
couvade 54–9

depression, and parenthood 94–5

education system, need for parenthood
   education 130–1

emotions
   and fatherhood 107, 112–13, 115
   and moment of birth 69–70
   problems of expressing 10, 35, 95–6,
     134–5
employment *see* work
'engrossment' 14

family
   changing structure 122, 126–7, 133–4
   social cycle 50
fatherhood
   changing attitudes to 76–9, 106–7,
     121–2, 128–9
   'couvade' symptoms 54–9
   as a cultural imperative 13
   depression 95
   development of relationship 107–10
   early reactions to 80–6, 87, 89, 96–7
   effects of working wives 23–5
   fears of 47–53
   and view of own father 85–6, 96, 121
feeding 90–1
financial costs, and fatherhood 48–50, 117

gender
   cultural 102–3
   definition of 17–18
   sensation of 71

Holland, home vs. hospital births 77
hospitals
   and births 77
   changing attitudes to fathers 77–8

Japan, home births 77

labour
   father's reactions to 63–5, 75
   'partners' 77–8
language
   and father's relationship with child
     104–6
   see also baby talk